WITHDRAWN

# Halfway to Heaven

## MAX SINCLAIR

77895

BETHANY HOUSE PUBLISHERS
MINNEAPOLIS, MINNESOTA 55438
A Division of Bethany Fellowship, Inc.

ACKNOWLEDGMENTS

Quotes from 'A Step Further' are used by kind permission of Joni Eareckson and Steve Estes. 'Never had to go this far', words and music by Jamie Owens, © copyright Lexicon Music Inc. 1975. Used by kind permission. All rights reserved.

Published in England by Hodder and Stoughton

Cover photo by Brian Osborne

Published by Bethany House Publishers
A Division of Bethany Fellowship Inc.
6820 Auto Club Road, Minneapolis, Minnesota 55438

Printed in the United States of America

---

**Library of Congress Cataloging in Publication Data**

Sinclair, Max.
  Halfway to heaven.

    1. Sinclair, Max.  2. Christian biography—England.
3. Physically handicapped—England—Biography.
4. Christian life—1960-    5. Suffering—Religious
aspects—Christianity.
I. Armitage, Carolyn.  II. Title.
BR1725.S468A34  1982    280'.4'0924 [B] 82-9587
ISBN 0-87123-258-8 (pbk.)

---

# FOREWORD

Woodland Hills
California
USA

Dear Max,

What a delight to have received your letter. I am thrilled to see your manuscript completed and I wanted to get back to you as soon as possible with my appreciation.

You really are a miracle – after suffering a broken neck, you are up and about walking! But what is an even greater miracle is your joy, not in spite of your disability, but because of it. You have learned to grab hold of your trial as an opportunity to display God's power through your weakness and that is a miracle to smile about!

Give my best love to your wonderful family and hugs to all the animals, especially that orphaned lamb. I think back on our visits with many, many fond memories.

Yours in His love,

Joni Eareckson

"God sometimes uses sorrow in our lives to help us turn away from sin and seek eternal life. We should never regret his sending it."

2 Corinthians 7:10 (Living Bible)

# INTRODUCTION

This is a story that could easily have remained untold. It came to be written only because of a remark made by a friend visiting me at a time when I was critically ill. He only stayed a few minutes but they were minutes that profoundly affected both his life and mine.

'When your feeling better you should write a book,' said James Casson. 'It is very obvious that Jesus Christ Himself is helping you through this devastating experience.'

My response was polite, but underneath I was thinking, 'If you knew how ill I'm feeling you wouldn't make impossible suggestions like that.' It was not until some time later that I realised the immense difference that the company of the living Christ made in facing suffering. It also dawned on me later that suffering experiences are more the norm than the exception.

James apparently left in something of a daze. He had seen his fair share of the world's suffering. But this was the moment God had chosen to ask a fine Christian doctor the personal question: 'How would you react if you were totally paralysed like Max?'

Within a few months James discovered he was dying of cancer. He had less than a year to live.

During that time he wrote a book: *Dying – the greatest adventure of my life.* In doing so he opened a window which has enabled many thousands to glimpse the goodness of God in the heights and depths of his personal pilgrimage homewards.

In sharing my own story, it is my prayer that any enduring thorn in the flesh God may have given you on your journey home, may be transformed from a source of irritation, to a cause for rejoicing. That kind of change needs a miracle. I am convinced we have a God who specialises in just this type of miracle.

# INTRODUCTION TO THE U.S. EDITION

Though the style and some of the vocabulary of this book have a certain English flavor, we feel that the story of God's grace and power in Max Sinclair's life is one that should be shared with an American audience. We believe that this strong testimony of one couple's faith and of divine intervention will forge another link in the chain between American Christians and our brothers and sisters in Christ across the ocean.

The Publishers

# CHAPTER 1

'Wake up Daddy,' insisted an eager, childish voice close to my ear. 'Wake up, it's morning.'

I opened a reluctant eye to see my five-year-old daughter looking severely at me from the side of the bed. She was just tall enough for her face to be on the same level as mine on the pillow. Her hair was tousled as if she'd only just got out of bed herself.

'It's not time to get up yet is it?' I remonstrated sleepily.

'Yes it is,' she said, stretching out her hand and tugging at my pyjama sleeve. 'We're going to stay with the Tollasts today.'

Of course. That was the reason for my early morning call.

'We've got to get ready.' Annie was exasperated at my lack of movement.

'Mummy's up, you know, and you've got to help me get dressed.'

'All right. How about putting your dress on and I'll help you with the zip.'

She put her head on one side, considering, then nodded and turned to go. At the door, she looked back warningly. 'Don't go back to sleep though.'

I assured her I wouldn't, and she padded off down the corridor.

The house had been awake for some time. Doors had started to bang even earlier than usual, and voices to rise above the whisper we tried to impose before 'proper getting up time'.

Our two girls were excited at the prospect of spending their first night away from home. They'd been preparing for days, packing and unpacking their suitcase and leaving very little out of it in the end. Now the great day had arrived. No wonder Annie was so bouncy.

9

'Daddy!' exclaimed an imperious little voice. 'You're asleep again.'

My eyes had been closed for barely a minute. I hadn't bargained for Annie clambering so quickly into her dress.

'My goodness, that was fast work,' I said approvingly, propping myself up on my elbow and trying to sound quite awake. She smiled shyly, pleased at her achievement and forgetting she was cross with me. I zipped up the little flower-sprigged dress Sue had put out for her the night before, and she skipped away as soon as the job was done, flinging a sing-song 'thank you' over her shoulder. She didn't have to worry now whether I got up or not.

I pulled myself into a sitting position and reached for my Bible. Normally Sue and I read together each morning, but today I'd been catching up on sleep after a speaking engagement late the previous night. Sue was up and downstairs before I'd left dreamland.

Opening our daily study notes, I flicked over the pages of the Bible to the appropriate place. I settled myself more comfortably against the pillows and began to read, continuing the habit of the larger part of my thirty-two years.

Brought up in a Christian family, I couldn't remember a time when God wasn't part of my daily life. One particular memory had always remained very clear in my mind. I was about five years old. It was the middle of an ordinary morning at home, and I'd been out amusing myself around the farm with my beloved dog, Moss. We must have made some exciting discovery, because I know I was anxious to tell my mother something when I burst into her bedroom, out of breath, not even having remembered to take off my muddy shoes at the kitchen door.

She was kneeling at the side of the bed, her face in her hands. She didn't look up, although she must have heard me. I stopped dead in my tracks with surprise. Normally, Mum would have been in the kitchen at this time anyway, and to find her here and so preoccupied was the last thing I expected.

Confused, I waited a few seconds at the door. My instinct

was to rush forward and pour out my tale anyway, but something in her quiet, solemn attitude stopped me. Would she turn and speak to me? It didn't look like it. What was she doing? Praying? Through my childish hurt, I understood that she might be doing just that, so I shouldn't disturb her.

I crept away, awed that my mother should prostrate herself before God like that when it wasn't even bedtime. Evening prayers were normal, but this was the first time I appreciated God was around in the day too.

'Were you praying this morning, Mum?' I asked as she tucked me into bed.

'Yes, Max. God is always with us and we can talk to Him any time.'

'So He listens in the day as well as at bedtime?'

My mother laughed. 'Of course He does.'

So I learned that God was present everywhere, all the time. And if He meant so much to my mother, He could mean the same to me. It was one of the most important lessons of my childhood.

The kitchen door slammed down below, and someone began to climb the stairs. Stomp, stomp across the creaking floorboards of our timber-built home. Naomi, older than Anna by about two years, appeared in the doorway, looping her hair behind her ear in a gesture of breathless impatience as she delivered her message.

'Mummy says you'd better hurry up or the breakfast will all be finished and do you want an egg?' This all in in one rush of a sentence.

'I shall be right down and yes, please,' was my reply.

'Morning,' said my daughter belatedly, and leant over to give me a kiss.

Breakfast was always quite a hectic affair in the Sinclair household. Feeding the dog, the cat and the children, not to mention ourselves, was no easy process. Fortunately it was a cheerful one for the most part. Naomi and I had evolved a system whereby she would put on the table all the things she could reach, and I would get down the packets of cereal and pots of jam from the higher shelves. Annie would usually entertain Ben, our youngest child and only son, while Sue, her long hair flying, raced from dolloping out cat food to scrambling eggs on top of our little gas cooker.

By the time I got down, order was already established and mine was the only empty seat. Sue was preoccupied with coaxing one-year-old Benjamin to swallow his cereal, and the girls had progressed to toast. My egg sat in its hat at my place.

'Well, are we all ready to leave?' I asked.

'*We're* ready,' chorused the two girls, and Annie rushed on eagerly. 'We've fitted *everything* into the suitcase.' Noddy – the name had stuck ever since Anna couldn't pronounce Naomi – was more sober. 'I've packed my notepaper so I can write you a letter.'

No one would guess they were just going to stay with a neighbour for one night.

'Did you ring Bob to tell him what time we'll be arriving?' Sue asked as I settled down to my egg.

'I haven't yet. I wanted to work out the best way of getting there first.'

It was an exciting day for us, too. We were going down to Devon for a very special occasion. The invitation had arrived in the morning's post several weeks earlier.

'Who's it from?' Sue asked excitedly as I searched for the signature. Neither of us recognised the handwriting.

'Bob Thomas,' I read. 'I haven't heard from him for ages.' Bob and I had been at school together, and I was best man at his wedding. Eagerly I skimmed through his closely-written letter.

'He's inviting us to a celebration dinner. A grand reunion of everyone who got married in the vintage summer of 1967 – five couples including us.' I looked up. 'Isn't that a great idea?' We'd all known each other quite well around the time we got married, but had hardly met up since. This year was our tenth anniversary.

Sue nodded enthusiastically, then looked doubtful. 'What about the children? We can't possibly take them all with us.'

12

That *was* a problem. And there was another one. 'It's on a Friday, too, and I'll be working.' I looked glumly at Bob's invitation. 'Looks like we'll have to say no.'

I began reluctantly to compose a letter of refusal in my head. It seemed such a shame to miss an occasion like this. In fact it was unthinkable.

'There *must* be a way we can manage it,' I said with determination. 'Let's try and work it out.'

I looked hard at the ceiling.

'Point number one,' I began. A plan of action was already forming in my mind. 'Ben is too young to leave with anyone so we'll have to take him with us.'

'Right,' agreed Sue.

'Point number two, we'll have to find somewhere for the girls to stay.'

'That's more difficult.'

'Well, who do they know well and really like to be with? Who is always thinking of creative, exciting things for them to do? Who lives in a house they love to go to?'

The ideal solution had just occurred to me. Sue looked puzzled and shook her head. Then her face lit up, and we exclaimed in one voice, 'The Tollasts!'

'Of course, the Tollasts,' Susie's eyes sparkled. 'The girls would love it.'

Robert and Anne Tollast lived in an idyllic little cottage only a short walk across the fields from us. Anne was a bouncy, vivacious type; fine-featured and a lover of spring blossoms and poetry. Robert was a youthful thirty years her senior, articulate and impressively well-read. He was a portrait artist. He'd painted Noddy and Annie's portraits for an exhibition, which was how our friendship had begun.

Sue went at once to the phone to speak to Anne, and soon that obstacle to our accepting Bob's invitation was happily out of the way. It only remained for me to arrange a day's absence from Hildenborough Hall.

Normally, this wouldn't have been difficult, but my responsibilities at the Christian Conference Centre where I'd worked for the last five years had recently increased; I was Acting General Manager while my cousin Justyn Rees was on sabbatical leave for six months, so I didn't feel I could just drop the reins and disappear. Moreover, there was a conference planned for that week, which I would be leading.

'I really ought to be there,' I said to Sue.

'Mac, I'm sure they can do without you for one day,' she remonstrated in her turn. 'Isn't Edward Smith coming to help lead that week anyway? He'll manage perfectly.'

Edward had been involved with Hildenborough long before I had. He was a competent leader and a good friend, and when I phoned he wouldn't hear of our missing the dinner.

So it was all arranged.

I pored over the map after breakfast, glad to note that we'd be able to travel on fast roads for most of the time. Nonetheless, the distance was considerable, and we couldn't reckon on covering it in less than six hours. I felt a little uneasy at the prospect of such a long journey, even though I enjoyed driving as a rule, no matter what the distance.

'Which car should we take?' I asked Susie as she stood whisking up a cake for the girls to take with them to the Tollasts. We were lucky enough to have two cars: a Citroen 2CV which Sue used as a 'run-about', and an old American convertible. The latter was the source of great entertainment at the Hall. Visiting teenagers were never satisfied until they had been for a drive in it, and since it was large enough to cram in a football team I would often oblige and take parties of wide-eyed, whooping passengers up and down the long Hildenborough drive.

'The Citroen would use less petrol,' said Sue, licking off a bit of cake mixture that had coated the top of her thumb. It was like her to think of the economics first.

'But then,' she added, 'it would take a lot longer.'

'And be terribly noisy. Ben wouldn't be able to sleep, and we'd have to shout to make ourselves heard if we wanted to talk.'

Sue smiled at my emphatic objection to the Citroen, well

aware that I would prefer to drive the powerful Plymouth Baracuda any day.

'Well,' she conceded, 'I think it's got to be the big car this time. Don't you agree?' She raised a teasing eyebrow, hardly needing to ask my opinion.

So it was decided. I picked up the telephone and dialled Bob's number. His wife Rachel answered with a cheerful 'Hello'.

'Rachel, it's Max here. Just to say we should be with you about six this evening, all being well.'

'Couldn't be better,' responded my hostess. 'The others won't be coming before eight, so you'll have plenty of time to change and relax after the journey. You haven't forgotten it's black tie?'

I laughed and assured her that Sue and I would be suitably dressed. We very rarely attended anything formal, and I'd had to borrow a dinner jacket and tie for the occasion. This had been greeted with great enthusiasm by my family, who pronounced it 'very becoming' despite its being a little small for my six foot two inch frame.

There was an hour to go before we set off, in which the cases had to be packed, the dog taken for a walk and the girls bundled to the Tollasts'.

The cases first. I ran up the stairs two at a time to join Susie in folding clothes and making sure we'd remembered everything we'd need.

'Just a *quick* walk with Sunny,' Sue warned as I sped down the stairs again. She knew how easily I lost track of time when indulging in one of my favourite pastimes.

Sunny, our golden retriever, was waiting for me down in the kitchen, her tail wagging expectantly, her eyes pleading and impossible to resist.

'Sunny dog,' I teased, lolloping with her round the kitchen and pretending I had no intention of taking her for a walk. 'There's no time for a walk today. We're off to Devon in a minute.' A tantalising reach for the handle of the back door. 'Stuart from the Hall is coming to look after you and I'm sure he'll take you out.' A second of silent expectation.

15

'Well,' I weakened, turning the handle. 'Just a quick run then,' and in a bound of frenzied excitement Sunny was through the open door and leaping off towards the woods.

It was a warm July day, hazy rather than sunny, with a damp freshness in the air after rain the previous evening. Everywhere was green and luscious. I crossed the drive and headed down the well-trodden path towards the valley. It was so quiet. I listened to the sound of my feet swishing through patches of long grass. So peaceful.

Sunny had disappeared. I stopped briefly and was surrounded by the silence. Through it I heard the tell-tale snuffling and tiny snaps of twigs which indicated that Sunny wasn't far away. Sure enough, round the next bend, there she was, racing off again as soon as she knew I was still following.

I came to the gate leading into the open fields and 'Happy Valley'. This was the nickname we'd adopted for the beautiful stretch of land ahead. A wide field sloping down into the folds of the valley, surrounded by hills doubling over each other in an endless variety of green. Beyond, the fields paled into a misty patchwork, dotted here and there with darker clusters of trees.

It was a haven. And the Creator who had painted such beauty had brought us to live in the midst of it. Little did we dream, when we prayed five years earlier for a 'house on the hill', that our prayer would be answered so abundantly.

At that time we were in Nairobi, and the job that had taken us out there a year before was just coming to an end. I'd been applying for others at every opportunity, because we both loved the outdoor life of East Africa and wanted to stay.

But it seemed that God had other plans. Justyn had already asked us to join him in the running of Hildenborough Hall, and as each door closed in Kenya we knew we were meant to go back to England.

The next problem was finding somewhere to live. The Hall was perched high on top of a hill, where there were very few houses, and although there were more down in the valley we didn't want to be isolated from the Hildenborough community. So we asked God to provide us with a house on the hill. I can still remember Sue's words.

'Lord, we know you have our return to England already planned. Please help us to find somewhere to live near the Hall so the children and I needn't be cut off from where Max is working. We'd like a house on the hill, Lord.'

When He gave it to us, it was like a final confirmation that we'd taken the right step. As I walked along the valley with Sunny that morning, I thought back to the extra-ordinary chain of events which enabled us to purchase Pepperland. It was as if the Lord had stamped a preservation order on it just for us.

We first heard of the 'quaint little old wooden house' through Quintin Carr, the Chaplain at the Hall who came out to Nairobi to visit his son while we were there.

'It's perfect for you two,' he informed us over a cup of thick Kenyan coffee in one of Nairobi's pavement cafes. 'Set way back from the road, and only a stone's throw from the Hall. Two elderly ladies live there at the moment, but I reckon . . .' He looked at us knowingly. 'I reckon they'll be out of there by the time you return.'

Sue and I exchanged questioning looks while 'Grandpa' stirred his coffee with unusual energy, obviously pleased with himself.

'That's what I'm praying for anyway,' he concluded in explanation. Sue and I exchanged another glance, wondering whether to comment. But Grandpa seemed to consider the conversation closed, launching into a different subject altogether and making no further reference to his 'prediction'.

We little expected that Grandpa's 'wooden house' would be up for auction when the time came for us to return to England. Sue discovered it first, having come back a little before me to prepare for having our second child. I was snatching a couple of weeks' travelling before throwing in my lot with Hildenborough, and Sue and I had agreed to leave looking for houses until I joined her.

17

But there was the perfect place, tucked away on the hillside and surrounded by bluebells. Sue couldn't let it pass us by, but she only had one phone number where I might be contacted. I was sleeping heavily in the tiny hostel in Jerusalem when she rang, having only arrived there that evening and planning to leave the next day. God wasn't going to let us lose what He was putting before us.

The very next afternoon I was striding through the bluebells, still recovering from my hasty flight back, but as certain as Sue that we'd found our future home. If we'd needed any seal on the matter, the discovery of the old pig sty in the overgrown garden would have been it.

'Oh look, Max,' Sue exclaimed, pointing excitedly at the broken-down sty. 'It would be perfect for chickens!' She had wanted to keep chickens for as long as I could remember, and here was her dream coming true without any prompting from us. God wasn't just providing a house on the hill, but the optional extras too.

'How on earth are we going to pay for it though?' Sue despaired as we wandered through room after room. 'It's so much bigger than the Orpington house, and the garden goes on for miles.'

'Well, we'll just have to see,' was all I could say, knowing full well that our old home in Orpington was unlikely to fetch a sufficient price.

But this too was in God's plan. We had to put down the money for Pepperland, and I was already well into my summer-long job of pulling down and putting together the ramshackle interior when a Christian couple came to see our old home.

'This is definitely what we've been looking for,' the husband said gladly as he stood in the living room. He seemed as certain about it as we had been about Pepperland. He put in an offer there and then for exactly the amount we'd had to pay for our house on the hill.

We couldn't look back now. There was no doubt that we were meant to be at Hildenborough.

I whistled to Sunny and turned back towards Pepperland.

There was still so much to do to improve the place. I had just completed my study, panelling and making box seats round the walls, and now there was the window to fit in the dining alcove. That wouldn't take long.

'Come on Daddy, come on Daddy,' voices greeted me excitedly as I opened the door.

At last, everything was ready. Three scrubbed children, two clutching teddy bears and the third sucking his thumb and surveying the world tranquilly from his mother's arms. One battered old suitcase containing somewhat incongruously our neatly folded evening wear, and another bulging with all the girls' belongings. The map, the car keys, the cake tin – mentally I ticked everything off, and at the last minute dashed to the drawer in my desk where I kept my driving licence. Something prompted me to take it on this journey. As I picked it up, I remembered the last time I'd carried it with me. I was driving a large double-decker bus-load of children on a day's outing and we'd had a minor accident when a car turned sharply left ahead and my emergency stop was just too late to prevent us from careering into the car in front.

We piled haphazardly into the car, the girls unusually silent now the moment of departure had come.

'It's only tomorrow we're coming back, isn't it?' asked Annie in a very small voice. Sue reassured her, telling her that time would pass so quickly they would hardly notice they'd been away.

'Good,' responded Annie emphatically, throwing herself back into the seat and staring resolutely out of the window.

Once we reached the Tollasts', their cheerfulness returned. Almost as soon as the car doors were open they were being called into the garden to admire the new sandpit and the last we saw of them was their running figures disappearing round the back of the house. With a furtive wink of thanks to our neighbours, we pulled out of the drive and set off.

# CHAPTER 2

Sue and I rarely had time together just to talk. Normally life with the children was so busy we had to rely on snatched conversation or sleepy chats before we went to bed. A long car journey with only one toddler who might sleep most of the way was my idea of a real treat.

It wasn't long before Ben's eyes were closing. His head nodded and he slipped down in his little safety seat, fast asleep. This was the unconscious signal for us to relax after the hustle of packing, and begin to enjoy the journey. Time seemed to stand still. My uneasy feelings about the drive evaporated as we embarked on a long, meandering conversation. The subject was our future.

'Would you really like to go back into Accountancy?' Sue quizzed me.

I had told her earlier that week that an old friend in a pleasant, small practice had repeated his offer of a job. He had made the offer before on several occasions and it was always in the back of my mind if ever I thought of leaving Hildenborough Hall.

'If I did go back into professional practice, Tim's job would be ideal,' I replied. 'But it would be a big change for all of us.'

'Mmm,' Susie mused. 'But why leave the Hall? Everything's going very well, and the plans for the future look terrific. Why think of leaving now?'

'It's not that I want to leave, my love. I'm just wondering how things will work out when Justyn comes back. I'm not sure I want to go back to the school's work with Pace.'

'Pace' was the Christian music group based at the Hall, whose reponsibility was primarily to schools and youth groups. I had been part of the team for five years now, and was feeling a little 'long in the tooth'.

'It was fine when I was actually playing in the group,' I

20

went on, remembering the thrill of standing before a crowd of young people, many of whom would be hearing the gospel for the first time.

'I don't think anything will quite compare to being used by God so . . .' I searched for the right word to express what I wanted to say. 'So . . . *immediately*.'

I paused, thinking back to our many concerts. The open-faced, searching young people, some excited, others troubled by what they were hearing. The endless questions, sometimes curtailed by the start of afternoon classes, sometimes lasting well into the night, thrashed through over cups of steaming coffee. The joy and release of a decision made, of Christ entering and filling a person's life. The exhaustion, yet exhilaration, of night after night in concert.

Even way back, when Justyn had only recently taken over the running of the Hall from his father, Tom Rees, and he and I alone made up the Pace team, God poured out His blessing. Through my trepidation and uncertainty, lack of talent and experience, He had spoken to the hardest of hearts. They were times I'd never forget.

But Pace had grown since then, and so had demand. It had become necessary for one person to be responsible solely for organising a schedule and ensuring that it was carried out. The task fell to me. I embarked on it with enthusiasm, but gradually began to miss being on the front line. Organising Pace just wasn't the same as being part of it.

'Do you want to go back to playing in the group then?' prompted Susie.

'No, not at all. The team's great as it stands, and – and I'm too old to get out my guitar again.'

A peal of laughter greeted this comment.

'Well it's true, isn't it?' I rejoined defensively, laughing despite myself.

'I don't know,' Sue teased. 'A little weathered for a teenage rock star perhaps, but . . .'

Our conversation dissolved into an exchange of playful accusations, punctuated by helpless laughter and anxious glances towards the back seat in case Benjamin was disturbed.

'But anyway,' I persisted eventually. 'I'm ready for something new. Leading the conferences these past few weeks has shown me all sorts of things. I'm much more excited about doing this kind of work. For one thing, I'm directly involved with people again.'

Sue nodded. Having shared with me the efforts of the past few weeks, she knew what I meant. At first I had felt daunted at the prospect of taking over from Justyn for a while, but in the event I had warmed to it not only as a challenge but as a real opportunity. Here was a chance to try a few of my own ideas.

And they'd apparently worked. The staff had been very appreciative of the few small changes I'd initiated, and I felt I'd gained their confidence. It was also a time when I felt absolutely in tune with God's calling. I knew I was out of my depth in many areas of the job but everything was turned over to Him, and He was making it good. But what was the next step?

'God has brought us this far,' Sue said philosophically when we'd considered every possibility without reaching a conclusion, 'so He'll take us on from here.'

'Right,' I agreed, mentally turning away from all we'd been discussing and relaxing in the security of that thought. 'What about a prayer?' Susie smiled, nodded and clasped my hand.

'Lord, you know the way ahead,' I began, 'and we have faith that you will show it to us and help us walk in it. Thank you that we can give our concern about the future to you. And thank you too for today's trip and the evening ahead.'

I stretched my arms out contentedly, keeping the wheel steady. God seemed so close. It was as if He was travelling with us in the car.

The route to Barnstaple took us through countryside we loved, including Salisbury Plain, which we travelled through frequently to visit various members of my family. The road between Andover and Taunton had fast stretches of dual

22

carriageway and we sped along, impeded only by the odd roundabout.

'Should be there in good time at this rate,' I said, glancing at my watch.

'Hey!' Susie cried out suddenly, breaking into the timeless feel of the conversation and stiffening in her seat. 'Look out! That Mini . . .' In front of us a white Mini had pulled out of the central reservation to cross over our carriageway. It was well ahead of the traffic flow so no one slowed down. But instead of accelerating the Mini stalled and completely blocked the road.

The two cars ahead of me began to brake at the same time as I did. We skidded wildly towards the Mini.

My unease of the morning reasserted itself, explained itself. I braced myself for what seemed inevitable collision.

But it never came. The Mini was untouched and we had stopped inches behind the first car. It didn't seem possible. Crazily strewn across the dual carriageway, the three cars were intact and without a scratch. A silent prayer of thanks escaped me.

'My goodness,' Susie said shakily, breaking the spell of shock which had held us motionless for several seconds. 'That was a near thing.'

In front of us, the drivers were gesticulating wildly to each other. In my rear mirror I could see the traffic beginning to tail back and one or two horns tooted impatiently. At last the Mini restarted and moved off, leaving the road clear.

My hand was unsteady as I put the car in gear. The cars ahead were already inching forward, and one by one, we pulled away.

'It's funny, you know,' I said after several minutes' silence. 'I had a feeling something like that might happen.'

'Did you?' Sue questioned in surprise.

'Just a notion. I picked up my driving licence, in case we might need it.'

'How strange. We nearly did.' Sue tried to brighten her voice as she looked round at Ben. 'At least old sleepy head didn't stir.' I glanced over my shoulder and grinned despite myself. Ben was still lolling in his seat, his thumb halfway to his open mouth.

We pulled into Bob and Rachel's driveway soon after five. The house was very impressive, red-bricked and tall with an unusually pointed roof. Our hosts were out and greeting us almost before I'd stopped the car.

'Welcome! Lovely to see you again. Come in, come in.' We were bundled through the front door into a wide hall with a polished oak floor and a profusion of flowers everywhere. Antique furniture peeped out from adjoining rooms, and a beautiful oak staircase ascended grandly in front of us.

'My, what a place!' I breathed appreciatively.

'Not bad, not bad,' Bob assented in his warm, deep voice. 'Lady Margaret has taste.' Bob was now manager of a vast estate owned by Lady Margaret. The house went with the job. I glanced at my old friend, wondering if the change in station had changed him at all. He looked the same – rather expansive waistline, friendly smile, balding.

'Got a beard then, Max,' he said as we climbed the stairs with our cases. I put my hand to my chin in what was now a habitual gesture, remembering that I'd been clean-shaven when Bob had last seen me.

'Bit of protective cover.' An urge to tease prompted me to add that his own hair was looking a little thin.

'Yes,' came the rueful reply. 'Can't stop it.' Bob had always been embarrassed about his baldness. I caught his eye and we burst into simultaneous laughter. It was the same old Bob.

'How was the journey down?' Bob asked later when we were comfortably settled with cups of tea in the informal surroundings of young Becky's playroom. She and Ben had quickly decided to be friends, and were happily engrossed with the contents of a big toy cupboard.

'Lots of traffic,' I began, and then related our near miss with the Mini.

'Thank goodness nothing happened,' Rachel exclaimed,

her small features unusually sober. 'The traffic's getting so much worse now the holiday period has begun.'

'There are jams miles long into Barnstaple at the height of the season,' added Bob. 'Actually it's not too bad if you know the short cuts round the local lanes – I'll show you a good way back for tomorrow if you like.'

'Good idea,' I said thankfully. 'Anything to avoid the main roads on a holiday Saturday.'

There was time for a walk before the other guests arrived. 'I want you to see the estate.' Bob confided, so we donned wellingtons and followed him into the garden.

'It's all so beautifully kept,' Sue commented as we made our way towards the surrounding parkland. 'How do you do it?'

'Shh,' Bob said mischievously. 'We've got a gardener.'

We strode through fields of sheep and dairy cows, past a new farm building complex Bob had designed himself, then into a little copse where Bob stopped. He waved his stick towards a huge mansion visible through a clearing.

'That's the House,' he informed us. 'Prince Charles has been there recently, you know. Lady Margaret has some impressive friends.'

We were speechless. The whole estate was like an unreal world – a step back into the rural England I thought had vanished in the 1930s. I thought of our own bit of 'country', where most of the population commuted to London each day for work. It all seemed very humble by comparison.

We were prepared now for a really special evening. Dressed in our finery, we must have made quite a picture sitting round the huge, exquisitely decorated dining table, with silver and cut glass winking in the candlelight. The butler – 'borrowed from The House' – completed the scene. Quietly, ceremoniously, he conveyed each course to our plates, while the ten of us laughed and joked and caught up on a decade of news.

It was surprisingly easy to pick up where we left off. Quickly relaxed in each other's company, we were soon reminiscing merrily about how we'd all met and come to marry.

Susie and I were fifteen when we first met. It was on a memorable winter evening when my brother and I threw our first, and only, party. Normally we were far too engrossed in the active life of the farm to spend time in such a social way, so this was a very rare occasion.

To our dismay, a couple of hours before it was all due to start, we discovered we were a girl short. We couldn't possibly have a proper party with uneven numbers.

'But we don't know anyone else,' wailed Bernard, convinced the evening was now doomed to failure.

'What about Simon Young?' I suggested after some desperate thought. Simon was one of the friends from boarding school expected that evening. 'Hasn't he got a sister?'

'Brilliant!' returned my brother. 'I'll ask him to bring her.'

And bring her he did. I clearly remember her shy smile and beautiful long hair as she stepped into our old farmhouse. The evening was saved – and a seed of romance sown.

We didn't see each other again until the following summer holidays when I went round to play tennis with Simon. Sue joined in, and soon became a regular partner. By the time the next holidays came round, I was going to the Young's house less to play tennis than to see Susie. The seed was taking root.

And then Bernard and I joined the Young's lively church youth fellowship. My great preoccupation at that time was the guitar, and Sue was flatteringly impressed by my musical efforts.

'Why don't you play for us sometime at a fellowship meeting?' she asked one day. I must have hesitated for she added as if to encourage me, 'I'll sing with you if you like.'

That struck me as a very good idea, and from shy beginnings we became quite a team. Sue had a lovely, clear voice and was delightfully unselfconscious when it came to singing. It was the following summer, when we'd both helped lead a children's mission, that Sue made up her mind.

'I think Max is the man I shall marry,' she told her mother. She seemed so convinced, Mrs. Young wisely held her peace.

My thoughts were nowhere near as clear. Life was hectic, and I was preoccupied with starting at University and booking a winter sports holiday. Had anyone challenged me, however, about my feelings for the girl who'd now become a fast friend, I'd have been hard put to find a sufficiently casual answer.

It wasn't until Spring 1965, five years after we'd met, that the subject of 'us' was raised. It was at the end of another mission we'd done together in Hastings, and this time it seemed very hard to anticipate separation.

'Come for a walk,' I suggested awkwardly to Sue on our last evening. I'd decided a policy meeting was called for. We clambered up to the cliff path, and walked a little way in silence.

'I thought perhaps we should have a talk,' I began hesitantly, staring at the sinking sun. Everything was bathed in its golden-red light.

'Yes, perhaps we should,' came the shy response as Susie kicked at a piece of turf.

'About us.' I couldn't catch her eye.

'Yes, perhaps we should.' She took another rather embarrassed kick at the ground.

'If we shared a few thoughts ...' I was beginning to wonder how one made a success of chairing this sort of policy meeting, when Sue looked up suddenly and smiled.

'Well,' she said. 'Tell me your thoughts about us.'

So I did, and she told me hers, as we walked along in the peace of the evening, the glassy calm sea below us. We both agreed that God seemed to have given us a priceless treasure. A quality and depth of friendship neither of us had previously experienced.

Because it felt so special we wanted to be sure it was from

God. We wanted this gift to form deep, sure roots and knew that for us, it would take time. I had another two years of University and three years Accountancy training ahead of me. So we hammered out a Charter to preserve our happy discovery of 'us' and ensure its steady growth.

Rule one was that we would always be completely honest with each other. We determined that no misunderstanding would be allowed to creep in and shatter our treasure. Every action, word and thought was to be shared, so we'd learn to trust each other in everything.

Rule two was an agreement to let the relationship develop in its own time. We knew that we shouldn't reveal our innermost thoughts all at once or our fledgling love might outgrow its own strength. Each stage of growth needed to be natural and unhurried in order to be secure. So we decided not to break the enforced separation of the term by travelling to see one another, and also agreed to limit our letter-writing. We had to wait two full weeks before replying to a letter, and then only write a few lines so as not to interfere with University working time.

By then, Sue was studying Geography and English at Kew, and the first of her exactly timed letters contained a newspaper cutting of us both singing in Hastings, and began, 'Dear Max, Just a brief line or two ...' Then followed no less than twenty-four pages in her neat, beloved handwriting.

Rule three was that we would not permit ourselves even the smallest physical expression of our love until we were sure we could commit our souls to each other for life. It was a self-imposed discipline we both took very seriously. We were convinced that true love could wait to find expression, and that waiting would bring greater reward.

More than a year later I took Susie out to dinner for her twenty-first birthday. Sitting on a bench near the cliffs of Fairlight we talked about getting engaged and I kissed her for the first time. We were married a year later and never once regretted our spring Charter.

Our anniversary dinner was almost over.

'Are you pretty settled at Hildenborough now, Max?' Rachel, sitting at the end of the table on my left, cut into my thoughts.

'Well,' I paused rather deliberately. 'Yes and no.'

'Whatever does that mean?' she laughed, and I explained something of the conversation in the car.

'So you see we feel we're on the edge of something new,' I finished.

Rachel nodded. 'You'll have to let me know how things work out.'

Little did I realise how soon, and how dramatically, our lives would change course. How could I know, as I stood up from the table at the end of the meal and walked over to admire the painting on the wall, that I would long in the months to come to be able to make such a simple movement? How could I foresee, as I sat talking on over a cup of coffee in the beautiful oak-panelled living room, all the suffering that lay ahead?

That evening in the country home in Devon was to have a very special place in my memory.

*    *    *    *    *    *

The traffic woke us the next morning. We weren't used to hearing the thunder of wheels on a main road so close to our bedroom. The noise intruded insistently on our sleep, until Sue gave me a nudge.

'Can you hear the traffic?' she whispered.

'Mmm,' I responded sleepily. 'Sounds awful.' I knew that, once awake, Sue would want to get up. It felt far too early. Opening my eyes a fraction, I squinted at my watch. It was 5.00 a.m.

Sue nudged me again.

'What about getting up and leaving early,' she suggested hopefully. 'We'll be home so much sooner that way.'

I sighed into the pillow. The bed was so warm and comfortable, and sleep not far away.

But it would be good to get an early start. We'd intended to breakfast with the others before leaving, but if we were on the road in good time we might miss some of the heavy traffic.

With a resigned yawn and a stretch, I rolled out of bed, dragging the sheet with me. Sue was up before me, rummaging for her jeans in the suitcase. Our evening clothes dangled from hangers on the wardrobe door, bringing to mind the candlelight and laughter of the night before.

'Heaven is a beautiful place,' I sang lustily as I disentangled myself from the sheet. That was one of the choruses we'd been singing in the car on the way down, and it popped into my head again just then, calling for a second rendering.

'Shush,' Susie shook her head at me. 'You'll disturb the others.'

I lowered my voice to a whisper, and set about getting dressed and putting our things together. Benjamin didn't wake as I picked him up in his sleeping bag. In a few minutes we were creeping down the stairs. Every creak and rustle was magnified in the stillness, and I half-expected our host to emerge, suspicious, from his room. But we reached the kitchen safely.

We breakfasted on cereal, and scribbled a note of explanation to Bob and Rachel. Outside, the traffic rumbled on. I wondered if we were taking credit too soon for our early start, and wished I'd pressed Bob the night before for his short cuts.

'Many thanks for a marvellous evening.' I finished the note and we slipped noiselessly out to the car. The sky was clouded and grey, and the early morning air was chilly.

'Looks like we won't be having the roof open,' I commented ruefully, looking vainly for a crack in the clouds that might let the sun through.

As always, we said a brief prayer before starting the journey.

'Lord, thank you for this new day,' Sue began. 'May it be a day in which we go with you and experience your presence.

You can see it is going to be a busy road, so we commit ourselves to you, in Jesus' name, Amen.'

'Amen,' I echoed.

It was 5.40 when I nosed the car out of the drive.

There was already a steady stream of cars heading towards Taunton. It seemed everyone had hoped to gain an advantage by starting early. I glanced at the speedometer. We were doing a bare 45 mph, and it looked like it would stay that way. I resigned myself to a slow journey, and settled more comfortably into the driving seat.

Susie was quiet, perhaps wondering about the children. They were often awake even at this early hour. I thought of the conference back at the Hall, and was glad I would be there to share the final day.

But we weren't destined to see the children or the Hall that day.

I didn't take any notice of the orange car at first. It was peeping out of the traffic coming towards us, as if to overtake. I expected it to drop back, since the road wasn't clear.

But it didn't. It strayed further over to our side of the road. There was no swerve, nor any other indication that the driver was out of control. But the car went on drawing further and further over, until it was isolated from the rest of the traffic.

I saw it clearly. A Ford Capri.

Everything was happening so quickly I couldn't take it in. Part of me was still waiting for the Capri to pull in, while my eyes confronted the horrific reality of the fast-approaching car.

It was coming straight at us.

Then at last I reacted, wrenching the wheel over in a desperate bid to avoid collision. This couldn't be happening. The world had gone crazy. My foot was hard on the brake, and a sudden dread that I would turn the car over gripped me.

If I could just drive it up the bank. . .

A flash of orange filled the windscreen, blinding me. Then, nothing.

\*    \*    \*    \*    \*    \*

I opened my eyes slowly. They felt heavy, as if I'd slept very deeply. I found myself looking at two feet with tennis shoes on, wedged awkwardly behind some car pedals. I looked at them for a long time, my mind blank and incomprehending.

My eyes travelled further up. Faded blue jeans with blood stains around the thighs, and two hands resting on them. The hands were white and curiously still.

On up, and I came across a face, staring back at me with tired, grey eyes. It was streaked with blood and dirt, and blood matted the fair beard.

Some time later, I realised I was looking at myself, my own reflection in the car mirror.

They were my legs too, then, and my squashed feet. What had happened? I struggled to make sense of what I saw.

Then I remembered. The journey, the traffic. The orange Capri and the flash of colour filling the windscreen.

Sue was kneeling beside me in the car, holding my head. She didn't seem hurt. Perhaps it was only my side of the car which had been badly damaged. The bodywork was twisted and broken around me, and bits of glass were everywhere.

'Susie . . .' I couldn't see her properly and wanted to find out if she really was all right. I could hardly say her name, let alone manage more. My voice seemed locked in my throat. I couldn't breathe properly. I could hear the dry, rasping sound of my breath.

'Max, I'm here. I'm not hurt, but you . . .' Sue's voice faded.

'Hold my head up,' I gasped. 'Please hold my head up.' I couldn't support it myself. There was a white hot pain in my neck, as if someone was twisting a knife into it.

Fighting for breath, I suddenly realised something else. I couldn't move at all. My hands were lifeless in my lap, and my feet and legs were locked in their crooked position. It was as if they didn't belong to me anymore. I couldn't even feel them. All I could feel was the searing pain in my neck.

Why couldn't I move or feel anything? My body was still there, but I was cut off from it. Was I going to die? If I was separated from my body, I must be going to die.

The thought of being so close to God in eternity filled me with a rush of joy. There was no room for fear. I was about to meet the One who'd created me, who'd walked with me all my life but whose face I'd never seen. Awe and wonder overwhelmed me. It didn't matter that my body was lifeless.

The pain in my neck meant nothing. I was on the final threshold, and longed just to cross it.

I began to pray out loud, feeling so near to the Lord it seemed that I was with Him already.

Sue leant over me and touched my cheek with her hand. Knowing I would be leaving her made me sad, even as I welcomed death. There were no words to say except the ones on my lips: 'I love you Susie.'

'I love you too,' she responded softly.

Around us, I could hear voices. Through the shattered windscreen I saw sympathetic, anxious faces. One man stood looking at us for a long time, his face grey and drawn. His eyes were distracted, and his hand trembled as he sipped from a steaming cup.

The car was at a crazy angle to the road, the boot up in the air on top of the high Devon bank. The soft roof had been ripped open, and a drizzle of rain found its way through on to us. All the time, traffic roared past, one car after another.

I heard Sue's gentle voice begin to recite verses of Scripture. The words washed over me like cool, refreshing water, and I soaked them up eagerly. Verse upon verse, filling me with peace and joyous expectation. The rain, the crumpled car, the unbearable pain in my neck – they were distant, part of the world I was leaving.

Far away, a siren began its haunting call. Nearer and nearer it sped, until the noise swallowed all other sound. No sooner had it stopped than I heard another, approaching quickly like the first. An ambulance didn't seem necessary really. Death was too close for that.

A uniformed figure looked through the hole in the roof. Sue was just repeating the precious words of Jesus: 'Lo, I am with you always, even to the end of the age.' They evoked a cheery response from the ambulance man.

'Don't worry, guv,' he called to me. 'She's never going to leave you.'

My only response was another rasping breath.

More people seemed to have gathered. The second siren must have been a fire engine, because a helmeted fireman came up and examined the door on my side of the car. Perhaps I would need to be cut out. I saw a policeman too. Sue didn't stop quoting Scripture, responding with a nod or shake of her head to concerned enquirers.

'We'll have to get a doctor out here, and quickly,' I heard one of the ambulance men say. 'We can't move him before we know the extent of his injuries.'

A woman came up and spoke to Sue, reassuring her that Benjamin wasn't hurt, just shocked and slightly cut from flying glass.

'Thank you, thank you,' was all Sue could say. 'His sleeping bag protected him,' she explained to me. 'The lady was so kind to take him. . .'

Waves of pain swept over me, blacking out my awareness of the hubbub around me.

A determined yank of the heavy Plymouth door revealed the doctor at last. With a friendly greeting, he leant towards us and looked closely at my neck. In a few moments, he had fitted a sort of collar around it. The pain seemed less sharp.

'All right,' he called over his shoulder. 'You can move him now. Go easy when you put him on the stretcher.'

An ambulance man took the doctor's place at the car door, and bent to ease my feet from under the car pedals. My limp body was inched out of the car on to a stretcher. It was strange to be moved and not feel anything. The ambulance was close to the car, and I didn't have a chance to see if the orange Capri was nearby. I wondered how badly it was damaged. The man with the cup must have been the driver.

Sue followed us into the ambulance, clutching our picnic basket and bits of luggage. Benjamin was in her arms. It seemed that life was continuing after all. A sense that everything would be all right now I was going to hospital replaced my expectation of death. I trusted God completely for what lay ahead.

# CHAPTER 3

I was only half-conscious during the ambulance journey. The siren roared its warning every so often, bringing me back with a jolt to the confines of the vehicle. When I opened my eyes, all I could see was the smooth metal curve of the ambulance roof. It was comfortingly real. The sound of traffic outside reassured me too, so normal and everyday. I felt very safe, listening to the changing tone of the engine as the driver manoeuvred the ambulance through the streets.

By moving my eyes painfully to the left, I could see Sue. For most of the journey, her head was bent in prayer. Near her sat the ambulance man who'd looked in on us through the broken roof of the car. He kept giving Sue worried looks, until finally he leaned over and placed a kindly hand on her shoulder.

'Are you all right?' His voice was very gentle.

I saw Sue look up, rather dazed, shaking her hair from her face.

'Oh yes,' she replied. 'I was just praying.'

The ambulance man seemed taken aback, and looked awkwardly down at his feet.

'Er, I see,' he said gruffly. 'Well, yes, that's a good thing to do.' He paused, and then raised his eyes with renewed concern as if he couldn't quite believe that Sue was as calm as she seemed.

'Really, I'm all right,' she assured him, smiling her thanks at his kindness.

He nodded, and gave her shoulder a comforting squeeze before taking his hand away and standing up.

'Well, if you need anything, just give me a shout. I'll be up with the driver.'

'Thank you.'

I could see Benjamin peering round Sue's shoulder. His face was covered in blood, and his little body shook with sobbing breaths. Not long ago, he'd been crying. The sound had reached me dimly, as if from a long way away. Tears still brimmed in his eyes, and he moved restlessly in a constant attempt to cling more tightly to Sue. She held him close to her, rocking him backwards and forwards.

My vision blurred, then cleared, then blurred again. Sometimes everything faded into an impenetrable distance, as if I was enveloped in a thick blanket.

The ambulance rumbled on for what seemed a long time. I heard the ambulance man speak again to Sue.

'Don't worry love, I've seen people a lot worse than your husband recover. Don't give up hope.'

His words washed over me, making little impression. I could barely grasp that I was the one referred to. He might have been talking about anyone.

At last, with a final shriek of the siren, we stopped. The ambulance doors were flung open, and a breath of cool fresh air swept over me. I breathed gladly. The sound of rapid footsteps grew closer, and the ambulance rocked as someone clambered in.

'Okay now, John,' said the someone as he approached my stretcher. 'You take that side, and I'll take this.' A white-coated young man positioned himself to lift me, and our kindly travelling companion came over to assist him.

'One, two, three, lift,' said the newcomer, and I

experienced that heady feeling of being suspended in mid-air as the men took the weight of the stretcher.

'Easy does it,' encouraged another voice from the open doors, while I watched the metal roof of the ambulance give way to a grey, rain-filled sky. My stretcher-on-wheels was tilted briefly as I was lowered to the ground, and I caught a glimpse of dull, concrete walls and a bright red sign saying 'Accidents and Emergencies'. I felt a sprinkle of rain on my face before I was wheeled briskly through some swing doors into the warm antiseptic atmosphere of the hospital.

The light was dim by comparison to outdoors, and since my vision was limited to the ceiling I couldn't gain much of an impression of my surroundings. The paintwork was white, aged to a yellow-grey in places, and I could tell when we passed a window because of the light reflected on the ceiling. The corridor echoed with the clatter of my mobile bed and the purposeful tread of the hospital staff.

With a final turn, I was wheeled into a small room with bright fluorescent lights running along the ceiling. Machinery seemed to take up most of the room. My bed was brought to a halt and I closed my eyes in relief. I felt dizzy from all the movement.

A friendly voice greeted me.

'Hello, I'm Dr. Hughes.'

I looked up at a young, serious face, bending considerately over my bed. The doctor introduced himself as the Senior Registrar.

'Hello,' I returned. My voice surprised me. It was hoarse and thin, and didn't seem to belong to me.

'We're going to take some X-rays first of all,' continued the doctor, 'then we'll take you through to the examination room for a few tests.' He spoke matter of factly and I wasn't sure if I was meant to respond.

'Thank you,' I said eventually.

I heard him give some instructions, and a bustle of activity ensued. One of the larger machines was rolled heavily nearer my bed, and positioned so that my head lay between two metal plates. Someone placed a hand on my forehead and I heard two dull clicks close to my ears. Then, with sharp decisive movements, the plates were repositioned, one coming lower over my face and chest. My forehead felt cold without the comfort of the hand.

I began to feel dizzy again and the room became distant. Dimly, I heard more slow clicks as the X-rays were taken. Then I was being wheeled out of the room and back into the corridor.

We reached a second door almost at once. The examination room. The lights were bright as before.

'The staff will get you ready,' Dr. Hughes told me as he passed my bed.

His voice rose and fell as he went by.

A nurse explained that they needed to remove my clothes before Dr. Hughes could examine me.

'Thank you,' I responded as before, grateful for all that was being done for me. Hazily, I watched various faces moving in and out of view, intent on the job of undressing me.

'Mr Sinclair,' the same nurse spoke to me again. 'We're going to have difficulty with your shirt. Would you mind if we cut it?'

I almost acquiesced, as seemed expected of me, when the full meaning of her question struck home. Cut my shirt? Why on earth should she want to do that? I would need it again soon anyway. Wouldn't I be going home shortly?

I didn't understand that she simply wanted to move me as little as possible, that my bloodstained, hampering clothes needed to be taken off quickly so that my injuries could be treated without delay. I didn't realise how seriously I was hurt.

Out of my confusion came a single, extraordinary protest.

'Nurse,' – this said with injured dignity – 'do you realise I've been on television in this shirt?'

The nurse looked at me in blank amazement, eyebrows high under the curls of her hair. She glanced down at her scissors, undecided whether to employ them or not, then turned and marched out of the room. Perhaps she's going to consult one of her superiors, I thought. I wondered whether she might think I was some famous film star in disguise.

She returned without the scissors. Not a word was said as she bent to ease the offending shirt from my shoulders.

At that point I was distracted by something new. I could feel her hands on my shoulders. What a comfort that was. It was the first time I'd felt anything during the whole process of my being undressed.

'Thank you,' I said as the shirt was finally removed.

'Just one more thing,' responded the nurse briskly. She picked up my hand from the bed and fastened a slim, milky-coloured band round my wrist. It looked as if it was made of plastic.

'There. Now we know who you are.'

This was my identification band. It seemed to seal my entry into the hospital, making me an 'official' patient. Still, in some strange way, I felt as if all this was happening to someone else and not me.

The shirt was the last thing to be taken off. With some embarrassment I realised I was now quite naked. I watched one of the other nurses go past with my clothes neatly piled in her arms, and felt helplessly unprotected. Wearily I closed my eyes. They felt swollen and sore, irritated by the glass which had showered down on me from the broken windscreen.

Something warm and damp was washed over my face. A flannel. It smelt refreshingly of soap, and felt good against my skin.

'Are you ready for a few tests, Mr Sinclair?' I opened my eyes to see Dr. Hughes beside me again.

My instinctive reaction to his question was to nod, but even before my mind registered the intention, I remembered I couldn't move my head. Summoning my energy for the effort of speech after all, I managed a small 'yes'.

'It won't take long,' the doctor resumed kindly. 'Could you try moving your fingers?'

I concentrated on doing as he asked, but couldn't locate my hands. The message to my fingers was blocked. I looked anxiously at Dr. Hughes, wanting him to tell me that he had seen some movement, but his face was impassive, conveying nothing.

'How about your arm,' he instructed next. 'Can you lift it off the bed?'

I tried to contract my muscles but nothing happened. It was as if my arm was no longer there. I wanted to look down and make sure that it was still part of me.

'I don't seem to be able to manage that,' I said as lightheartedly as I could.

'Try wiggling your toes now.'

I fixed my eyes determinedly on the ceiling. Somehow I knew that my efforts were useless.

'All right,' said the doctor. 'Let's try something else. Tell me if you can feel anything.' He took something out of his pocket and moved down the bed. I waited expectantly for some sensation.

'Nothing?' queried my examiner a few seconds later.

'N. . .no,' I stammered in reply, uncertain what he was doing and what I should have felt.

'How about this?' He bent over me and stretched his arm across to my left shoulder. I felt a sharp sting just below my neck.

'Yes, yes, I can feel that.'

'Good, and this?' Another sting on my shoulder. It felt as if I was being jabbed with something painfully sharp, and a note of remonstrance entered my voice as I reported that I could certainly feel that. The doctor grinned.

'I was pricking you with a pin,' he informed me. Then, without further explanation, he moved away.

The examination over, I was covered with a sheet and left without disturbance for a while. I didn't reflect then on the implications of the tests. It was as much as I could do to keep pace with what was happening immediately around me. The thought that I might be paralysed, permanently or otherwise, didn't register at all.

I was surprised, when the Registrar's voice addressed me again, to find myself in such strange surroundings. For a moment, I couldn't understand why I wasn't in my own familiar bed at home. Then the memory of what had happened returned with a jolt. Dr. Hughes was speaking, and I tried to make sense of the words.

'We'll stitch the gash in your head, Mr. Sinclair, and then we'll put you into skull traction. I have to ask your permission to do that. It simply means fixing a small gadget on your head. Is that all right?'

I had no idea what skull traction meant, but supposed it was necessary.

'Fine,' I responded, puzzled too by the doctor's reference to a gash in my head. How had that happened?

A nurse approached with a tin basin and some cotton wool in her hands. Her starched coat rustled as she walked, and something metal clinked at the bottom of the basin. She stood behind me and began cleaning my injured head.

'Is it bad?' I asked timidly.

'Oh, not really. Nothing a few stitches won't cure.'

I was silent a moment.

'I didn't realise it was there.'

The nurses responded to the appeal behind my words.

'You hit the side of your head against the car roof,' she said gently. 'But it really isn't very bad. It won't take a moment to stitch it.'

I saw the top of Dr. Hughes' head as he bent, concentrating on putting the stitches in. It was soon over, and the nurse informed me of the next step.

'We need to shave your head, Mr. Sinclair. Only a little, so your hair won't get in the way of the tongs.'

I was wondering what the tongs might be when I heard the noise of the razor and felt its roughness against my scalp. I could feel it moving down the centre of my head, and imagined my hair peeling away. I was left feeling lost, another little bit of my normal self gone.

When the razor had done its work, Dr. Hughes reappeared.

'Mr. Sinclair,' he began in his characteristic, business-like way. Being called by my surname all the time made me feel even more alien in this strange hospital environment.

'I'm going to drill two small holes in your skull. It won't be painful, so don't worry. We'll give you a local anaesthetic first.'

Holes in my skull? I had visions of a huge drill boring into my head, and tensed myself in anticipation.

Something icy cold was sprayed on to my bare scalp. I heard what sounded like a dentist's drill but the vibrations that resounded in my head seemed worthy of something much larger. For an endless few seconds, I was conscious only of grinding, reverberating noise.

Abruptly, it was over. I listened to the high pitch of the drill fading into the distance. An irregular sound of metal on metal replaced the drilling noise, and the occasional jolt to my head told me that the 'tongs' were being fitted.

I wished I had some idea of what they looked like, what they were for.

Dr. Hughes announced that the job was done. There was a new tension in my neck, as if something was pulling it backwards. I asked the nurse if she could describe the traction so I could at least have a picture of it in my mind.

'Well . . .' she began doubtfully, trying to assess whatever was on my head.

'The tongs are about this shape and size,' – she made a semi-circle with her thumb and forefinger, holding them a couple of inches apart – 'and are fixed into two small holes on the top of your head. They grip like any other tongs really and are attached to a piece of string which runs over a pulley at the top end of your bed. The weights are placed on the end of the string.'

'The weights?'

'They're to hold your neck taut so the misplaced bone can heal.'

'I see,' I murmured, although I didn't really understand what had happened to my neck. I remembered how I hadn't been able to hold my head up after the accident, and how very painful my neck had been until it was supported by the surgical collar, but no one told me I had broken it.

The nurse obviously saw my puzzled look, and said brightly, 'The tongs are very precious, you know. They are made of silver, so you'll have to take good care of them.'

I laughed with her, the tension momentarily dispelled.

Just before I was wheeled out of the examination room, two filled bags were placed either side of my face. They looked like bean bags disguised as small pillows, but in fact were fairly solid. They lay close to my cheeks, holding my head in place. Obviously I would have to put up with the view of the ceiling for a while yet.

The journey back down the corridor was different from the first. I felt subdued, awed by the strange new hospital identity I seemed to have assumed. We went more slowly, and Dr. Hughes held my head all the way, keeping the traction steady. I was told that I would now be transferred to the main hospital across the road, the Queen Elizabeth Hospital. This would entail another short ambulance journey. I thought of Susie, wondering what she'd been doing all this time.

'Will my wife be coming?'

'Oh yes. She's waiting in Reception for you now.'

The corridor opened out, and I strained my eyes sideways, eager to catch sight of Sue. But I could only see the tops of people's heads, and that in a very small bit of the wide reception area. Sue would have to come up to us if I was to see her at all.

We stopped near the reception desk while the main doors were propped open. Still looking about me as much as I could, I saw Sue at last, approaching hesitantly with Benjamin in her arms.

I grinned widely. I must have looked quite alarming with all the machinery around my head. Sue glanced uneasily at the traction, and back to my puzzlingly cheerful grin. Our eyes held in silent communication. Hers were calm, despite the pallor and tiredness of her face, and I know she felt God close to her as I did.

The next moment I was being wheeled out into the fresh air again. Dr. Hughes still held my head in position, and gave precise directions when it came to lifting me into the ambulance. Sue followed with little Benjamin and our bits of luggage.

The journey was over very quickly. This time I was only dimly aware of being taken through more corridors and into a small, quiet room. Several people surrounded me to ease my limp body from the stretcher on to a bed, and then I was left on my own except for one nurse who sat beside me. She seemed to know that I couldn't cope with the demands of conversation. She simply said she was there if I needed anything.

I couldn't tell how much time passed before the swing doors to my little room opened again. It was Dr. Hughes. He'd come to put a drip in my arm. I watched the contraption being set up beside my bed: a tall metal stand, an upturned bottle, a tube extending downwards. I was faintly surprised that I was going to be fed intravenously. I still couldn't gauge how ill I was.

As the needle penetrated my arm, I yelped an involuntary 'Ouch!' Dr. Hughes looked at me quickly, as if he hadn't expected to hurt me. I was still too confused at that point to remember that a few hours earlier I had been unable to feel the jab of a pin below my shoulders.

The stillness of the room was like a balm. I might have slept, except that the traction was becoming more and more uncomfortable. I couldn't understand why the weights seemed so heavy when I had hardly noticed them at first. I supposed it would take time to get used to them, but as the minutes ticked by they only seemed to get heavier. I felt as though someone was pressing my forehead hard into the pillow, oblivious of solid resistance from underneath. In that calm room, I was soon in a turmoil of throbbing pain.

'Nurse,' I whispered at last, unable to bear it any longer. Her face appeared above me at once.

'Is there anything you can do to lessen the pull of the traction? My head feels ready to burst.'

44

The nurse put her hand comfortingly on my shoulder, where I could feel it, and regretfully shook her head.

'I wish I could,' she said gently. 'But the weights must stay constant. Your bed will be turned soon and the pain will ease then.'

I could do nothing but wait. My head ached and swam, and waves of blackness passed in front of my eyes. I had no idea why or how my bed was to be turned. I just longed for the relief it would somehow bring.

The dim quiet of the room was suddenly broken by footsteps and the thud of the swing doors being pushed open. A doctor and another nurse came up to my bed, and someone set some machinery in motion. I heard the whirring noise, and then became aware that one side of my bed was slowly lifting, tipping me up so that I faced the far side of the room where the wall met the ceiling.

The release of the pressure on my forehead was immediate. The sandbags had been taken away as the bed was turned, and my cheek now lay against a pad of some kind that was fixed to prevent my head from dropping sideways. I leant against it gratefully, relieved beyond words that the traction weights seemed lighter from this angle.

Around me, the nurses were busy, easing pillows from under my body and plumping them up vigorously before sliding them back.

'There you go,' one of them said as she smoothed my sheet in a final gesture. 'See you again in a couple of hours.'

I thanked her warmly, and supposed that two hours was my appointed time for staying in one position.

Freed from pain and my mind clear, I began to take more notice of where I was. I could see shelves and some large filing cabinets along the far wall, and the swing doors at the end. They had round windows in them like portholes, and were painted dark blue. As I looked at them, they swung inwards and Sue appeared. She hesitated before approaching the bed, as if she wasn't sure how she might find me.

My gladness at seeing her must have communicated itself immediately, for she took the last few steps quickly and leant over to kiss me. She drew up a chair as closely as she could to the bed and sat down.

'I'm fine,' I said in answer to her unspoken question. My voice was still dry and hoarse. She smiled ruefully.

'Does your neck still hurt badly?' she asked in a low voice.

'No, it's much better. It seems all right when it's held straight.'

Sue nodded. Her eyes were drawn irresistibly to the contraption on my head.

'You look funny with all that on,' she said. I couldn't help laughing. I felt as if I must look grotesque, but Sue had managed to find some humour.

'What about you?' I continued a little breathlessly.

'I'm fine too. You'll never guess what's happened.'

'Tell me.' There was always something good to hear when I was told I wouldn't guess it.

'Auntie Alys was at the Hall when I phoned this morning to tell them about the accident.' Alys Moss, with her silvery hair and smart dress, was a familiar figure at Hildenborough. Affectionately known as Auntie Alys, she was the one everyone turned to for comfort or advice. 'I don't do anything really,' she'd say modestly when asked about her role at the Hall. 'Just talk to people.' But just that always did so much.

'She thought of something to help straight away,' continued Sue. 'Did you know Roger lives near here?' I'd met her son on a couple of occasions, but had no idea where he lived. 'Well she phoned him up to tell him about us, and he came over at once and offered to have me and Benjy to stay for as long as we like. I've left Ben sleeping there now.'

That really was evidence of God's care. It warmed me that someone should be so willing to help.

'And he arrived just at the moment I was beginning to give up,' Sue added. 'I'd been trying to get Ben to sleep in the children's ward, but he wouldn't settle down. I didn't know how long we'd have to wait, and hadn't managed to find anyone I knew in the area to turn to – and suddenly there was Roger with his big bear hug and comforting words. I just let him take the luggage and followed him.'

'That is wonderful,' I acknowledged gratefully. 'So you'll be nearby.'

'For as long as you're here,' Sue assured me. Neither of us knew how long that would be. We were silent again, just looking at each other. I wanted to take her hand and squeeze it comfortingly, but of course I couldn't. I wondered if she was holding mine. I couldn't feel it, and wished she might touch my shoulder or my cheek.

'And Noddy and Annie are all right at home,' went on Sue, sensing that I'd want to know even though I couldn't get my thoughts together enough to phrase the questions. 'They'll stay with the Tollasts for the time being.'

'That's good,' I said. It was becoming more difficult to make sense of what Susie was saying.

'It seems like I'm looking at you from the wrong end of a telescope,' I told her. Her face appeared very small and far away.

'I'm still right beside you,' came the clear reply. Then, 'Shall I read to you? I've got my Bible with me.'

I could think of nothing better. 'Please,' I said appreciatively, my voice so thin I wondered if she heard me. But soon I was hearing precious words from Scripture again. The words washed over me in much the same way as they had done in the crumpled car after the accident. They spoke to me of God's presence and continuing care, and surrounded me with His love.

I hoped it wasn't too long before I was next turned, because the traction weights seemed heavy again, and the pad I leant against was digging into my cheek. The pain increased slowly as before, until my cheek felt raw and my head throbbed unbearably.

'Sue,' I had to interrupt her reading. 'Would you ask the nurse if they'll come to turn me soon?' I didn't know how I would stand waiting any longer.

I heard Sue talking to the nurse, who explained to her

47

about the turning. 'She says soon, Max,' she reassured me, looking anxiously at my tense face.

But it seemed hours before they came.

'Where are they?' Sue asked the nurse helplessly. I heard her say something about numbers of staff, and that she'd do it herself if she could manage on her own. At last, the footsteps returned and the bed was swung back to its original position. The relief was momentous. The soft, kind sandbags were placed either side of my face once more, and the many pillows plumped up and rearranged. I almost wept my thanks.

This process was to become all too familiar. The weight bore down on my forehead again as I lay on my back, and when I was turned on my side – whether to the right or to the left – the pad ate into my cheek. The second hour was always the worst. The first was a merciful respite, and I could never believe the pain would intensify so much before the next turn. When it did, it seemed as if I'd been enduring it for ever without relief.

One thing I shall always be thankful for: I never spoilt the first hour in anticipation of the second. God protected me from such psychological torture, asking only that I cope with the present.

After Sue had gone that evening, I felt very alone, lost in the whirl of the day's events. My bed was tilted so that I faced the other side of the room, and I lay staring at a square of twilit window. The night stretched ahead, long and uncertain.

Normally, I would turn to my Bible for comfort or inspiration at such times. But the simple act of picking up the book, opening it and reading it was denied me. Then I thought of the nurse.

'Nurse,' I cleared my throat and tried to moisten my dry lips so as to form my words better. 'Have you got a Bible there?'

'Well no,' she replied apologetically. 'But I can soon find one if you want.'

'I'd like you to read me a little if you wouldn't mind.'

'Oh, of course,' came the willing response. 'It would be a pleasure. Just hang on and I'll ask someone to fetch one.'

She went quickly to the swing doors, and I heard her making her request to someone passing by.

'It'll be here in a minute,' she reported, returning to her stool.

Sure enough, a Bible was brought within a few seconds.

'Where would you like me to read?' the nurse asked, rustling the pages in anticipation.

'Could you find Psalm 40?' I suggested. I'd been reading a psalm a day since Justyn left for his sabbatical leave, and I'd reached number 40.

There was a more urgent rustling of pages.

'I think it's in the middle somewhere,' I offered helpfully.

'Ah yes, here we are.' She found the Psalm and began reading.

'I waited patiently for the Lord;
He inclined to me and heard my cry,
He drew me up from the desolate pit,
    out of the miry bog,
and set my feet upon a rock,
    making my steps secure.
He put a new song in my mouth,
    a song of praise to our God.'

Each word that was spoken evoked a response in my own heart. Lying in that hospital bed, I was stripped of everything except my faith in the Creator and Saviour of the world. But my faith meant more than anything else. It gave me a rock-like security, despite the 'desolate pit' of my present suffering. I could rejoice with the Psalmist even as my neck strained against the traction. The simple, overwhelming *fact* of God's love came home to me more emphatically than ever, and overflowed in warm thankfulness, 'a song of praise'.

'Blessed is the man who makes the Lord his trust . . .'

In no way did I question what God was doing. I knew

that He was infinitely to be trusted, and the peace which
came from that trust made me feel 'blessed' indeed.

'I have not hid thy saving help within my heart,
I have spoken of thy faithfulness and thy salvation . . .

Do not thou, O Lord, withhold thy mercy from me,
let thy steadfast love and thy faithfulness ever preserve
    me.'

I remembered the many times I had spoken of the saving
power of Christ, of the love and faithfulness of God. Never
was I more convinced of the truth of what I'd stood by, and
never had I been in greater need of the care and protection
of a faithful God.

The nurse's voice became warmer, more emphatic, as she
neared the end of the Psalm.

'But may all who seek thee
    rejoice and be glad in thee;
may those who love thy salvation
    say continually, "Great is the Lord!"

As for me, I am poor and needy;
    but the Lord takes thought for me.
Thou art my help and my deliverer;
    do not tarry, O my God!'

There was a short silence.

'Isn't that wonderful?' the nurse finished softly, her voice
reverent.

'Wonderful,' I echoed. 'That was just what I needed to
hear.' I felt a new closeness to the nurse, a warmth in sharing
God's Word. It helped make the room seem less lonely.

I slept fitfully that night, disturbed by the alternate hours
of nagging pain and the regular turning of my bed. I suffered
too from a raging thirst. Every so often I would ask the
nurse for a drink of water, but each time she reminded me

that the drip provided the liquid I needed and that I wasn't supposed to take anything through my mouth. She would moisten my lips with a damp cloth, but the dryness afterwards seemed worse than ever.

Somewhere in the middle of the night, she asked me if I would like a glacier mint. She thought it might help to alleviate my thirst. I accepted gratefully, but soon wished I hadn't. The mint stuck to my dry mouth like cotton wool, leaving me with a parched, sickly taste that lasted well into the next day.

Slowly, imperceptibly, the morning light crept into the square of sky at my window. One moment it was dark, the next palely grey, and then a washed, translucent blue. I was glad the night was over, yet nothing changed in my little room. No breakfast was brought to start the day, and no one came to wish me good morning.

Later, Sue returned. She read to me a little, and then simply sat quietly in her chair beside the bed. I was glad just to know she was there.

The sour taste from the mint still hadn't gone, and my teeth felt coated in an unpleasant film. Sue had brought a little parcel of things she thought I might want: my Bible, the old volume of Daily Light verses I'd carried around since the day it was given to me, a comb. She'd also brought my washbag, and I knew it contained a toothbrush among the other bits and pieces.

'Sue,' I began, finding it difficult to ask like a child for help. 'Do you think you could brush my teeth?'

'Of course, Mac.' Sue rummaged for the toothbrush. 'Is there something I could use to put water in?' she asked the nurse, who had just taken over from my companion of the previous night.

'Yes, have one of these basins.' I heard a cupboard door sliding open, and the clatter of a tin like the one used when my head was being stitched.

'That'll be fine,' Sue said, and went over to the cupboard near the doors.

When she'd filled her basin, and spread a towel under my chin, she set to with the toothbrush.

A strange embarrassment crept over me. Sue was doing for me what she used to do for the girls when they were small, and what I was doing for Benjamin with his two new teeth only the other day. So basic, and yet I could no longer manage it myself. I felt humiliated, and disturbed suddenly by the thought that I might often have to be given such help.

My feelings were further complicated by the fact that Sue was the one helping me. It was the wrong way round somehow. Normally, in my role as husband, *I* looked after *her*. For the first time it came home to me that I could no longer fulfil that role.

'Hey,' Sue reprimanded gently. 'You're not opening your mouth wide enough.' Obediently, I opened my mouth a little more, and concentrated on enjoying the freshness of the toothpaste.

Other incidents that day brought back those disturbing thoughts. The air in the room became stuffy, and I had to ask for a window to be opened. The nurse did that for me. I needed a handkerchief, but couldn't blow my nose myself so Sue helped me. I could do nothing for myself, and each request hurt my pride a little more. Whereas during the night I hadn't worried about asking the nurse to wipe my face, it now seemed a humiliation and I tried to suppress my desire for the cool refreshment of the flannel.

In the evening, we were visited by some young people from the local church. They sang in the main ward beyond the portholed doors, and then grouped into my little room to share a hymn especially with us. We joined in the worship with enthusiasm. Sue held her hymn book above my head and I even managed to sing a little.

A sense of normality was restored in that moment. Things didn't seem so bad after all. I chatted with the young folk afterwards as I might have done to visitors at the Hall, and felt almost cheerful.

It didn't last.

After they had gone, and Sue had left me for the night, I

was seized by a desolation I hadn't known until that moment. The hurts of the day flooded back, and I saw the horrifying possibility of my being paralysed for the rest of my life, confined to a wheelchair, dependent on someone for everything. I struggled to hold back the pictures of a future existence that tumbled into my mind, but it was as if the lid of a box had been opened and the contents released irrevocably. I couldn't shut them back out of sight.

I saw the dipping field behind our home, and the trampled path leading to it. I'd walked along there many times with the dog or the children or simply by myself. I remembered the warm smells of the earth in summer, and the crisp, breathless cold of winter. I would never walk there again.

I saw the children tumbling about on the garden lawn, playing hide and seek among the furniture inside, running away from me when it was time to go to bed. I remembered the whoops of delight during games of Cowboys and Indians when I, the horse, carried a brave, childish hero on my back. I wouldn't play like that again.

I saw myself in a wheelchair, Sue feeding me, pushing me along, washing me. People looking down at me, standing awkwardly as if I embarrassed them.

I cried, the tears welling and overflowing silently.

The nurse leant over and wiped my face, brushing the tears gently away. She said nothing and I hardly noticed her, still seeing the ever-changing, ever more desolate pictures. The Hall where I'd spent five committed years. The empty lounge. Would I ever speak there again? What about my God-given ministry?

I thought of all the activities Sue and I enjoyed together: the games of tennis in thirsty heat, the skiing in winter on white-clad slopes, the horse-riding, the walking, even digging the garden. Sue would be on her own in all these things from now on.

I felt bereaved. I mourned the loss of my body, of my past.

Out of the confusion of images came a prayer, a wordless

reaching out to God. The box yielded a final gift, the words of a verse of Scripture, a Psalm.

'Thou dost show me the path of life;
in thy presence there is fullness of joy,
in thy right hand are pleasures for evermore.'

It was as if God held those words in front of my eyes specially. I knew the verse well, from Psalm 16, but suddenly it was infused with new meaning.

I needn't worry about anything as long as God was with me. He was the source of all life, of everything I'd ever needed or would need. His presence was all that mattered, I could entrust Him with my life now just as I had done long ago when I first gave myself to Him.

That moment of still, peaceful recognition was one of eternity. I felt prepared to accept whatever lay ahead because I knew God was in control. Still I wept for what was lost. As I lay tied within my paralysed body, the traction weights pulling relentlessly and my mouth parched and swollen, my tears spilled on to the pillow until at last I slept.

# CHAPTER 4

News of the accident travelled fast. I was lying flat, half dozing, when my first visitor arrived that Sunday afternoon.

'Tim!' I exclaimed as the ruddy, smiling face of my old friend Tim Giles appeared above me.

'Hello Max. Just thought I'd pop down and see how you were.' Considering he lived up in Surrey, this was no small gesture. I was touched that he should have come so far, but didn't make the connection with the seriousness of my condition. I was just glad to see his familiar, friendly face. We'd been to the same school, trained together as accountants in the City, and he was now a member of Hildenborough's Management Council.

'Did you drive down in your Morgan?' I couldn't imagine Tim without his sports car.

'Of course. Top down all the way!'

We chatted easily, as we might have done on any ordinary occasion. It was almost as if nothing had happened. He stayed only a few minutes, but the cheerfulness of his company buoyed up my spirits.

It was quite different with my father.

He came early one evening, while Sue was still at the Mosses' putting Benjamin to bed. I recognised his characteristic, heavy tread before he actually came into view.

'Hello Dad.'

I hadn't seen him for over six months. Somehow, with my going away to boarding school and then to University, we had never managed to forge those essential links which might have held through subsequent years. We saw very little of each other now.

He managed a smile as he looked down at me.

'How are you doing, Max?'

I could sense his distress beneath the controlled exterior. His shoulders were tensed up, as if he held his hands tightly clasped behind his back.

'I'm fine really,' I said. 'They're looking after me very well.'

Dad nodded, his face grave.

'You needn't worry about all the ins and outs with the police and the insurance and everything,' he said matter-of-factly. 'I'll take care of all that.'

'Thanks.' He had always been a stalwart support in a time of crisis, thinking of everything and sorting out all the practicalities. I wanted to ask how he was, but he went on before I could say anything.

'And don't worry about Sue either. I'll make sure she and the children are all right while you are here.'

This time a lump in my throat held back my words. Financial security came high on Dad's list of priorities, and I knew he would do all he could for Sue. I remembered how disappointed he'd been when I gave up Accountancy, worried that I would not be able to support my family on the income from the Hall.

There was a pause, and Dad looked away from my face at the traction, the drip, the invalid bed. Wordlessly, he leant over to smooth my hair back from my forehead.

With one movement, the old childhood relationship seemed to revive. Memories flooded back. I was in bed with a miserable bout of measles, and the same paternal hand was cooling my hot forehead. Again in bed, this time with an agonising combination of chicken pox and shingles, and Dad was beside me, reassuringly smoothing back my hair. I always felt better when he was there.

And now, I drew the same consolation from his presence. I felt closer to him than I'd felt for ages. And yet a new sense of helplessness flooded over me, taking away the adult dignity I'd retained with Tim Giles. I was the sick child again.

'I can't stay long,' resumed Dad, the control in his voice breaking a little. 'They told me not to.'

He took his hand away and stood back from the bed.

'I'll see you again soon,' and he was gone from view. I listened to his retreating footsteps, and felt lost without his comforting hand.

I spent most of those first few days in a state of semi-consciousness. There were no meals to give the day its familiar pattern, so I had nothing to help me keep track of time. The changing light at the window indicated whether it was night or day, but after a while I couldn't remember how many days had passed.

Perhaps it was the third or fourth day that I woke to find Justyn and his wife Joy at my bedside. Joy was holding tightly on to Sue's arm as if for support.

'J . . . you've come all the way down from Northumberland.' Regret filled my voice as I realised he'd had to come back. There was no one else to run the Hall. 'I'm sorry I've landed you back in it.'

Justyn made a gesture to stop me speaking. 'Don't worry about that. How are you feeling?'

'Not bad just now. Looks like I'll be here for a while though.'

'Don't worry about the Hall,' J repeated. His firm, broad chin was set with determination. 'We were missing the place anyway, weren't we Joy?' I knew he was just saying that to reassure me. They'd both needed a break. Joy's small, attractive features were expressionless, frozen. As Justyn turned to her, she made an effort to smile.

'We'll manage, Max,' she said at last. 'You just concentrate on getting better.'

A few more minutes, and they turned to go.

'J,' I called urgently as the two girls moved out of sight. He came back at once.

'I . . . I just wanted to ask you about Susie.' J nodded understandingly as I continued, almost pleading. 'Is she really all right, do you think? She's so calm, but I don't know.'

'It does seem hard to believe, but she's fine.' I clutched gratefully at his assurance. 'She's been comforting us, for goodness' sake! I think it's a miracle – the Lord is looking after her in a special way.'

'Thanks,' I breathed. If Susie had been anxious, and had managed to hide it from me, it would surely have been evident to our two closest friends, so Justyn's words put my mind at rest.

It wasn't until weeks later that I heard more specifically about God's upholding of Susie. On the day of the accident she had to watch me being moved from place to place without even knowing how seriously I was hurt. She had to cope with a fretting Benjamin, the worry of letting people know what had happened, the problem of where to stay and how long she should prepare to be away from Noddy and

Annie. Everything was uncertain, and when the real situation was finally revealed to her by Dr. Hughes, it was the biggest blow of all.

'He looked very solemn when I went in to his office,' Sue recalled when she felt able to tell me what Dr. Hughes had said. 'I knew he was going to say something serious. There was a nurse with him who came and stood beside me while he spoke. Perhaps they thought I might faint or something.'

The doctor came straight to the point and told Sue the results of his examination. I'd broken my neck and was completely paralysed. 'I couldn't take it in at first, and then he sort of explained it a bit more, saying it was likely you'd be in a wheelchair for the rest of your life. He said it would mean a big change in our lives, and although there might be some recovery I should face the possibility of none at all.'

I was shaken, thinking how devastating this must have been for Sue. But she reacted in the most incredible way.

'I just told him we were Christians, and that God would see us through,' she told me simply. 'I don't know how that must have sounded to two professional people, but they were the words that came first to my mind. I felt this overwhelming reassurance that God knew about everything, and somehow had it all in control, even as I was crying inside at the thought of you being paralysed.'

It was amazing that she should have been so calm, so sure at such a moment. I marvelled at her faith, and at the God who upheld her.

I gradually got used to the hospital. Instead of lying in silence when there was no one but the nurse with me, I made a few efforts at conversation. The more I got to know those who sat watchfully at my bedside, the more I felt able to relax. Some of the old self began to find its way back, and I even took to cracking jokes in my more cheerful moments. Sue teased me about this, accusing me of thinking I was back at the Hall and nowhere near a hospital.

Sue stayed with me as long as she could every day. She always looked fresh and pretty, as if she was making a special effort for my sake. She never usually wore perfume, but from somewhere found a flower-scented one which surrounded her with a light fragrance and disguised the antiseptic smell of the hospital.

Sometimes she brought Benjy, when there was no-one to look after him at the Mosses', and then she'd dash in just for a few minutes before taking him for a walk round the hospital in the pushchair. We both agreed that he shouldn't come in with her to sit, as he would certainly be frightened at seeing me in such a strange predicament. The receptionist downstairs, June, was willing to entertain him for the odd ten minutes. She'd grown very fond of him since that first day when she'd soothed him and washed the blood from his face while Sue made urgent phone calls to family and friends.

One morning, not many days after the accident, I was told I had progressed sufficiently to be taken off the drip.

'How would you like to try a cup of tea?' Dr. Hughes cheerfully enquired. Tea! My mouth watered in anticipation.

'Oh, yes please.'

A nurse was despatched to carry out the order, but panic suddenly seized me.

'How am I going to *drink* it?'

Dr. Hughes laughed and explained that a special straw would be provided, flexible in the middle so it could be bent from the cup to my mouth. 'You'll see how easy it is.'

Sue took over with ceremony when the nurse came back with the tea, placing the straw so I could hold it in my mouth. She had to tip the cup slightly so the bent straw didn't block the liquid completely. It worked! I swallowed with delight the warm, fragrant tea. Never had it tasted so good!

The consequences weren't quite what I anticipated, however. My stomach hadn't had to cope with anything for five days or so, and the intrusion of the tea was more than it could manage. It rejected it decisively. I was upset and embarrassed. Once again I could do nothing to help myself, and had to watch the nurses change the linen deftly, rolling me very slightly to ease the sheet under my body.

'Don't worry,' Dr. Hughes reassured me. 'You'd have been lucky to get away with it! You'll soon be able to manage.'

The drip was removed anyway, and psychologically a milestone was reached. I said to myself I felt better.

That afternoon, I was transferred to the main ward. It was a simple matter of being wheeled through the portholed doors which led to the larger ward. Sue walked beside me, sharing my excitement at this evidence of progress.

I liked my new surroundings at once. The room was light and airy with fresh, lemon-painted walls. I could smell flowers, and out of the corner of my eye I saw a huge vase of coloured blooms on a small side table. The nurses approached in welcome, chiding me merrily for having been anti-social for so long in the little side ward. I felt almost euphorically well.

From my tilted vantage point I could see to the other end of the ward, where tall French windows opened out on to a sunlit garden.

'Hey,' I said in surprise to Sue, 'I thought this was at least the second floor, but we're right on the ground.' My view through the little window in my side ward had been simply of sky, so I'd assumed I was quite high up.

'And look. There are patients out in the sun.' I could count at least three beds beyond the French windows. A longing to be in the fresh air and feel the sun on my face possessed me.

'Sue, please find someone to help push me outside.'

Sue looked doubtful, but nodded. 'Don't get your hopes up too much though,' she warned as she disappeared.

A few moments later she came back with one of the nurses.

'I'm sorry, Mr. Sinclair, but we can't let you go out just yet. It's better that you're not moved again for the time being.'

'But', Sue began after a pause, sensing my disappointment, 'couldn't we wheel the bed *very* carefully?'

'I'm afraid not, Mrs. Sinclair. We must take one step at a time.' Her voice was kind, but didn't allow further argument.

I looked at the patients outside enviously. I didn't feel too ill to be moved, but since permission had been so firmly refused I had to assume there was reason for it. I didn't suspect my life could still be in danger.

Then the pins and needles began.

At first it was an almost imperceptible tingling, which I noticed one day during a session of physiotherapy. Since my promotion to the main ward, an energetic physiotherapist had come regularly each day to exercise my limbs, contorting my arms and legs into all sorts of positions to prevent the muscles tightening up.

'All this exercise is making my arms tingle, you know,' I informed my hard-working friend.

'Is that so?' she replied. 'Well, that's no bad thing.'

She didn't say any more then, but when I complained the next day of the tingling having increased and become quite painful, she paused in what she was doing and spoke emphatically.

'That's a *good* sign, you know.'

'Is it?'

'It means your muscles are waking up.'

She returned to the job in hand, vigorously moving each of my arms in turn, bending them at the elbow and wrist and stretching them out from the shoulder.

'At this stage,' she continued, 'you *should* be getting some sensation back in your arms, and movement too.'

'Movement?'

The word escaped from me incredulously. This new information took a moment to sink in.

'You mean,' I said hesitantly, 'I'll be able to move my arms?'

'If we keep working,' was the warning response.

This put a completely different light on the pins and

needles. With new enthusiasm, I made every effort to follow the instructions of my physiotherapist.

'C'mon,' she would encourage. 'You *can* move that arm. You know you can.'

It seemed impossible. Try as I might, I couldn't manage a hair's breadth of movement for myself.

'Don't be silly,' my undaunted physio would chide when she thought I was giving up. 'Of course you can do it.'

And one afternoon, I did. Sue testified to my right elbow lifting the tiniest bit off the bed.

'What did I tell you?' cried my triumphant physio.

I was so thrilled I continued to practise long after the official physiotherapy session was over, determined to improve the achievement. By the end of the evening, tired out but exuberant, I had moved my arm half way up my chest. I felt I had made a tremendous leap forward. With movement returning, it would surely not be long before I was up and about, and able to go home.

In the meantime, I had to make the most of being confined to a hospital bed. During the week of my stay, I'd got to know the staff quite well, and their cheerful company made a difference to the atmosphere of the ward. Some were especially considerate in their efforts to make waking hours less tedious. I slept most of the time, but welcomed any distraction when I was awake.

Nurse Thomas, a young student nurse, became a particular friend. 'I've got a surprise for you,' she said one morning after she'd changed the sheets on my bed. 'Close your eyes now.'

Amused, I did as I was told.

'Okay, you can look.'

She was standing beside me holding a large album open for me to see. Carefully arranged on the pages were various dried, pressed flowers.

'Hey,' I said admiringly. 'That's quite something.'

There was a pleased little grin on her face.

'I thought you might like them, being as you're a country person.'

'Of course,' I laughed, remembering our conversation the previous day. We'd discovered a mutual appreciation of the outdoors, she being a wild-flower enthusiast and I a lover of the open air. I was touched by her thoughtfulness. I looked more closely at the collection and discovered a few flowers that I recognised.

'Those really are lovely. How did you get them to press so well?'

She launched enthusiastically into detailed explanation of how she'd compiled the book. Her descriptions of the countryside in which she'd found the flowers were so vivid I could almost imagine my having been there too. For a moment it didn't matter that I couldn't go outside because the outside was being brought to me.

I had barely seen half the album when the Ward Sister came over and enquired with a twinkle in her eye why my sheets were the only ones changed in the ward so far. With a hasty assurance that she'd be back to show me more, 'if I wasn't too bored', my friend renounced the wild flowers and turned once more to her pile of sheets. The Sister clucked her tongue and raised her eyebrows, but failed to disguise the smile in her eyes.

My friend also treated me to the contents of her photograph album, and entertained me with the stories behind the pictures. I'm sure the other patients must have wondered how ill this newcomer really was, hooting with laughter with the nurses!

There were about a dozen patients in the ward altogether. It was an orthopaedic hospital, and my neighbours were bedridden like myself, so none of us could 'visit' each other. I only ever saw the patient in the bed immediately next to mine.

He was an elderly man, lying in what seemed to be an awkward and uncomfortable position on his back. For the most part, when I was turned towards him, he lay still and quiet, only rarely turning his head in my direction. Our eyes met for the first time when I'd been in the ward a couple of days.

'Hello, I'm Max Sinclair.'

'How d'you do,' was the rather formal response. His voice was low, and he seemed to have to make an effort to speak.

'My name's Walter, Walter Finch.'

'Glad to meet you.'

There was a pause.

'What happened to you then?'

'I was in a car accident, about a week ago.'

'Ah, I see. I fell down the stairs and did something to my hip. Can't walk. Nuisance.'

'I'm sorry.'

'Not a bad place, though, this.' He stretched his neck backwards on the pillow, as if it was causing him discomfort.

'The staff are nice.'

I agreed.

He moved his head uneasily, mumbling something about getting stiff. Eventually he settled so he faced away from me, and our conversation came to a halt.

We never exchanged more than a few words at a time. We shared opinions on the hospital food, what we could see of the weather, and occasionally on how we were feeling. He introduced me to his wife, a quiet, round figure who smiled shyly and volunteered even less conversation than her husband.

I was content myself not to have to make too much effort to talk. It seemed to demand a lot of energy.

My brother Bernard visited me soon after my arm began to move. When he arrived, I was busy doing my exercises. I had progressed to the point of being able to lift my arm up over my chest to my neck, but I was still trying to master the technique of bringing it back down again. The physiotherapy session that morning had yielded some movement in my wrist, and I was now discovering that I could 'walk' my arm back down my chest using my wrist. It was a slow and tiring business, but at least it worked. I could now both lift and lower my arm.

Bernard was obviously disturbed by the unusual state in which he found his younger brother, but made every effort to appear relaxed. He was gratifyingly impressed by my achievements.

'You go on like that and no one will believe you were paralysed,' he said warm-heartedly. His concern showed in quiet enquiries as to how I was feeling and whether I was being well looked after.

'Do they feed you enough?' he asked with a twinkle in his eye, knowing my usual large appetite. 'You don't need anyone to bring you slices of bread in the middle of the night to stave off the hunger pangs?'

We both laughed, remembering our school days when Bernard used to smuggle hunks of bread into my dormitory, concerned that I needed some extra sustenance or comfort.

We weren't alike at all in appearance, although we both had bushy ginger beards. Bernard was broader than I was and viewed the world from behind a pair of glasses. Now, with our respective families, we lived fairly separate lives, but had followed almost identical paths until we were married, going to the same school and University, studying the same subjects and even being articled to the same firm of Chartered Accountants.

'How's the farm?' I asked, not doubting that the response would be enthusiastic. Bernard had finally returned to his first love, farming. I envied him in many ways. We'd both grown up convinced that there was no better life than that of the farm. Where else could we spend all day outdoors, eat the fresh produce of our own fields, ride our own horses, be alone or with friends as we chose?

'It's fine, just fine,' came the reply, and I was being told of some of the latest developments when another visitor was announced.

'A policeman, Max,' Nurse Thomas whispered warningly.

Sue had told me the day before that the police wanted to get an official statement from me about the accident. A youngish officer approached, clip board in hand and his hat clasped firmly under his arm.

'Mr. Sinclair?' he asked politely, stopping a few paces from the bed.

'That's right.'

'You're expecting me I believe. Oh, thank you,' to Bernard who drew up an extra chair.

'This is my brother Bernard,' I explained.

'How d'you do.' He sat down and studied his clip board. 'I'm sorry to have to ask you to go back over what must be a painful memory . . .'

'That's all right,' I interrupted, glad to be feeling clear-headed. 'I'm only sorry you're stuck with the job of writing it all down. I haven't quite progressed to holding a pen yet.'

The policeman didn't know quite how to take this, whether to commiserate, or to respond in the light-hearted tone in which I'd spoken.

'Well,' he said, clearing his throat and shifting his position in the chair. 'You don't have to worry about that at all, sir. I shall ask you some basic questions about the accident, and if you would be so kind as to answer as simply, clearly and accurately as you can we should be through this in no time.'

He leant back in the chair, and took a pen out of his top pocket.

'First of all, can you tell me the exact time you set off in the morning.'

'We got up at five – the noise of the traffic outside woke us – and were on the road by about quarter to six.'

'So there was a lot of traffic?'

'Yes, everyone seemed to have decided to set off early.'

'When did the accident happen?'

'Quarter of an hour, twenty minutes after we'd set off.'

'Can you tell me exactly what happened?'

I could remember the morning's events with astonishing clarity. I saw again the steady stream of traffic and the orange Capri pulling out ahead.

'It all happened so suddenly. One minute we were driving along quite normally, and the next the world was turned upside down. The Capri seemed out of control. The chap must have fallen asleep at the wheel or something.' I described my feelings and reactions in detail, and the policeman wrote busily.

'Was the road wet?' he asked next.

'No, I don't think so. It didn't start to rain until after the accident.'

It was curious how I could look back and relate the events of that terrible morning so coolly, almost impartially. It seemed a thing of the past. In fact, I was never troubled by recollections of that day, even in my dreams.

Eventually, the policeman was satisfied.

'Right then, sir, if you will just sign this to verify it's correct, we can call it a day.'

He realised his error as he was leaning forward to offer me the pen.

'Oh, but of course . . . I should have . . .' He blushed a deep red, cleared his throat and began again.

'I'll read your statement over to you, Mr. Sinclair, and perhaps your brother could sign it on your behalf if it's all in order.'

So we did just that, the policeman looking relieved when Bernard had put his name to the document.

'Thank you for giving up your time,' he said finally, standing up and placing his hat back under his arm.

'Not at all. Thank you.'

Bernard offered to see him out, but was assured he needn't bother. The last I saw of my questioner was his stiff, uniformed back.

It was towards the end of the first week that Mum decided to come over and help look after Benjamin. She and Dad were divorced just before Susie and I were married. That had hit me very hard. I never realised before how unhappy they'd been, how completely communication had ceased between them. Living in Malvern now, and able to give her time where she saw a need, Mum was another of God's answers to unspoken prayer.

I was asleep when she arrived that afternoon. She must have stood beside me for several minutes before I woke. Her dear face was white and so utterly sorrowful my heart went out to her.

'C'mon Mum,' I said, seeing her rooted to the spot. 'Give me a kiss. I won't break.'

She half laughed, half sobbed as she leant carefully over the tubes and machinery to kiss me.

From then on, she and Sue took it in turns to look after Ben or come and sit with me. Sue would tell me what she'd been doing since she last saw me, read aloud a little perhaps, or just stay quietly beside me with her hand on my shoulder. Mum was more active, concerned that everything possible should be done to make me feel comfortable. She washed my face regularly, and combed my hair. And one morning she brought in some cream to rub into my skin because she said it was looking dry.

'Goodness me,' exclaimed Sue when I told her about this latest attention. 'What will she think of next.' I wasn't sure whether she thought Mum was fussing a bit too much, or whether she was feeling cross because she hadn't thought of the cream herself.

The day after Mum's arrival, Dr. Hughes paused during his busy daily round and came up to speak to me.

'How are you feeling today, Mr. Sinclair?'

'Not too bad, thank you,' I gave what had become my standard reply. I was tipped up on my side, and the pad was beginning to feel hard and uncomfortable.

'Good,' nodded the doctor, thrusting his hands deep into the pockets of his white coat. His stethoscope hung on his chest with an air of gleaming importance.

'Have you heard of Stoke Mandeville hospital?' he asked unexpectedly.

'Well no, I haven't.'

'It's in Buckinghamshire, and has the best spinal injuries unit in the country. We're going to transfer you there next week. It's far better equipped than we are here to treat an injury like yours.'

The best spinal injuries unit in the country. It all sounded very impressive.

'They like to take patients as soon as possible after injury,' continued Dr. Hughes informatively, 'which is why you won't be here much longer. I can assure you that you'll be in the best possible hands.'

'Yes. Thank you,' I mumbled, not sure whether I felt excited or apprehensive at this new prospect. It was encouraging to think I was going to be given specialist treatment, but I was just getting used to my bed and the folk at Exeter. A move seemed a bit daunting.

'Oh, and one other thing,' Dr. Hughes tossed over his shoulder as he turned to go. 'We're going to try and get a helicopter to take you there, so don't worry about the journey.'

That was even more impressive. I was going to be given real VIP treatment. Perhaps it wouldn't be so daunting after all.

Nurse Thomas dashed over as soon as the doctor had disappeared. 'Are you excited, Max? There's no better place for you to be, you know, and you're very lucky to get in. They give priority to emergency cases, and there's a huge waiting list.' By the time she'd finished telling me about all the wonderful facilities at this famous hospital I was convinced that a great honour was being conferred on me.

Both Susie and Mum were thrilled at the news.

'Just goes to show it was worth John ringing up so often,' Sue said grinning broadly.

'John ringing up?' This was the first I'd heard of Sue's cousin acting on my behalf.

'Yes. As a doctor he knows all about Stoke Mandeville and is convinced it's the best place for you. Dad thinks so too.' Sue's father was a doctor as well, and I could guess he'd been on the phone to Dr. Hughes along with John.

'Well I'm so glad their recommendation has been taken up,' Mum put in before I could offer any protest. 'It's marvellous.'

In the afternoon Sue rang the hospital to find out where she could stay. 'Apparently there's a hostel specially provided for visitors and there's plenty of room for us. It's just across the road from where you'll be.'

'She'll be in to see you at crack of dawn,' laughed Mum.

'And,' Sue rushed on, the tone of her voice suggesting she'd left the best news till last. 'The lady who looks after the hostel says Stoke Mandeville is lovely, right in the middle of the country.' She imitated a country accent, holding an imaginary telephone receiver to her ear. 'You'll love it here.' Laughing in delight. 'That's what she said.'

I was beginning to imagine a veritable mansion, Georgian perhaps, in the middle of vast expanses of green country.

Was I the only one going though? Would Walter Finch and the others stay on in Exeter? I looked across to the sad old man in the bed next to me.

'You're the only spinal injury patient we have here,' Nurse Thomas explained when I asked her about my apparently unique privilege. 'Stoke Mandeville couldn't do any more for the others than we can do ourselves.'

'I'll miss it here.' I felt quite tender towards the place now that I would be leaving it.

'Oh, go on with you.' Nurse Thomas chided as she arranged a profusion of roses in the vase beside my bed.

That evening, Sue brought her writing paper to my bedside and we composed a letter together to Noddy and Annie. They were staying with Sue's parents in Hastings, and we'd already had reports of the fun they were having on the beach and playing in Grandpa's boat.

'Daddy is being moved to a much better hospital,' Sue said out loud as she wrote. 'We shall be away for a bit longer, so you will have to look after Pepperland until we come back. I am sure you will have a lovely time with Uncle Simon and Auntie Sue.' Sue's brother had offered to move his whole family to our house on the hill while Sue stayed with me. That way the girls could have the stability of home once their two-week stay in Hastings was over. All the children got on like a house on fire, so we knew they'd be fine.

'It's wonderful how everyone is rallying round,' I

commented to Sue after she'd told me of Simon's suggestion. 'So much to be thankful for.'

And now there was Stoke Mandeville to look forward to.

# CHAPTER 5

August 3rd dawned bright and clear-skied. The helicopter was due to arrive first thing, so breakfast and my daily blanket bath were more hurried than usual. Sue had packed up my few belongings the night before, and promised to be at the launching pad to wave me off.

My first disappointment of the day was the news that an emergency case had demanded the use of my helicopter.

'Nasty accident, apparently,' Dr. Hughes told me as he checked over my notes for the last time. 'I'm afraid you'll be travelling in the ambulance after all. Shouldn't be too bad. It's a lovely day for a journey.'

There was nothing for it but to resign myself to a more humble means of transport. An ambulance didn't have quite the style of a helicopter, but it would get me there just the same.

I didn't reckon on it being such an old vehicle. As I was carefully eased into position along one side behind the driver, I looked up at bubbling and cracking paint, with suspicions of rust peeping from behind.

'Been on the road a while, this,' Nurse Thomas said disapprovingly as she settled herself on the long seat opposite me. 'I'm told it's got a new engine though.' This last to encourage me, I think. One of the other nurses from my ward scrambled in to join us and gave me a broad grin.

'All set? We'll be in here for several hours but it'll be worth it.'

'I'm fine,' I assured her. I did feel better than usual, cheered by the sunshine and the prospect of the day. Even my head was fairly clear.

The engine roared. Susie called cheerfully from outside.

''Bye Max.' I pictured her with little Ben in his papoose peering over her shoulder. 'Have a good trip. Mum and I will be just behind in the car.'

The doors were slammed shut and we were off.

Little did I realise as we built up speed on the open road what an agonising journey this would turn out to be. At first I enjoyed watching the sun dappling the roof, but as the ambulance grew progressively hotter and stuffier I began to wish the August weather had let us down instead of providing such a blistering day. Wafts of smoke from the driver's cigarette choked any remaining freshness in the confined vehicle, and soon I was feeling decidedly nauseous.

My two companions tried to entertain me with descriptions of the passing countryside, and little anecdotes which would have made me laugh had I not been feeling so awful. As my responses grew more infrequent and monosyllabic, they lapsed into silence until my only distraction was the occasional rather tuneless whistle from the driver.

It seemed like we'd been on the road for hours, although it couldn't have been more than two or three, when Nurse Thomas leaned over and suggested to the driver that we stop for a cup of tea. I sighed with relief at the thought of a few moments of stillness.

'Could you open the doors?' I asked almost desperately as we drew to a halt. A waft of warm air with a cloying mixture of dust and traffic fumes barely displaced the stuffiness of before. Someone produced sandwiches, but I couldn't face the thought of food.

The nurses understood how uncomfortable I was. Nurse Thomas wiped my face gently with a fresh-smelling flannel.

'Perhaps a sip of tea might help,' she said kindly.

My mouth was so dry I accepted a little, but soon wished I hadn't. We'd barely started on the road again when I was helplessly sick.

'Don't worry, Max,' Nurse Thomas spoke soothingly as she rearranged my pillows and bundled the soiled linen into a bucket. 'He'll drive carefully so you won't feel so bad, and we can give you an injection to help too.' One injection, and then a second, didn't seem to make much difference. I lay in utter misery, longing for the journey to be over.

More than seven hours after we'd set off, the ambulance turned into the drive of Stoke Mandeville hospital. As I was finally lifted out, my head throbbing and the old blackness dulling my senses, I suffered my second disappointment of the day. Someone seemed to have pulled down the Georgian mansion, and replaced it with rows of army barracks. Stoke Mandeville was nothing but huts.

*     *     *     *     *     *

Inside, the antiseptic hospital smell greeted me. In a swaying rush, I was wheeled along corridor after corridor. Skylights in the roof screamed brightness as we passed underneath, and I winced painfully. Down a little side corridor and then we burst into a pocket of noise and glaring light. Music, voices, a television all vying to be heard. This surely couldn't be the ward.

But we'd stopped, and through the hubbub I heard Nurse Thomas answering someone's rapid questions. 'Yes, that's right. Maxim Sinclair. We had a bad journey.'

'Mr. Sinclair?' A nurse bent over my bed. 'How do you do? I'm Sister Clements and in charge of this ward.' I was too bemused to respond.

'I'm sorry the journey was so long,' the Sister continued sympathetically, 'but we'll soon have you settled in here now.'

She straightened and called commandingly over her shoulder. 'All right. Will you get ready for lifting?'

Three broad young men approached and towered ominously above me.

'We're going to transfer you to a ward bed,' Sister Clements explained. 'Don't worry, it'll be very quick.' She explained briefly what would happen, but I was so frightened at the thought of being lifted I was deaf to her words. Couldn't they roll me like they'd always done in Exeter? Where was Nurse Thomas?

But already the men were bending, and Sister Clements clasped my head firmly. The next moment I was suspended in mid-air, totally disorientated and instinctively wanting to put out a hand to steady myself. Because I couldn't feel anything, it didn't seem I was being held at all. I yelled in fright, and closed my eyes tightly against the spinning ward.

'Well done,' Sister Clements said smilingly once the manoeuvre was completed.

Sick, dizzy and stunned, I couldn't return her smile.

For the next few minutes, doctors and nurses busied themselves round my bed. Blood samples were taken, urine samples. My skin was examined closely for the pressure sores I'd been warned could develop so easily if I lay in one position for too long. I wouldn't be able to feel them, and the skin could break without my knowing it. Pillows were positioned and repositioned. The traction weights were checked, and my eyes and mouth examined with a tiny torch light. Even an X-ray machine was dragged over to my bed to complete the examination.

All the time, the noise of the ward throbbed behind the orange curtains that had been drawn round my bed. There must be scores of people, and each with a radio or cassette player. The sound seemed magnified in my aching head, and I longed for the quiet of Exeter.

'We've got to go now, Max.' The soft voice of Nurse Thomas surprised me close to my ear.

'H . . . have you?' A lump caught in my throat. The thought of losing my two friends overwhelmed me.

'Now that you're settled, we're expected back.' I didn't feel settled. I felt ill and small. The lights were burning my eyes, and my head swam.

'Sue will be here soon,' Nurse Thomas continued gently, sensing my distress. She touched my shoulder in farewell. It was as much as I could do to say goodbye, and a choked 'Thank you'.

As I listened to their retreating footsteps, my eyes blurred with involuntary tears. My last link with Exeter was gone, and with it, all the distant optimism of the morning.

I was barely conscious when Sue and Mum arrived later that afternoon. I know they sat either side of me, very close, as if to shield me from the bustle around. I heard Sue say something about the hostel being fine, and the countryside beautiful, even if the hospital wasn't all we'd expected. I couldn't take in even that small comfort.

It was a long time before I got used to my new environment. The first few days were a blur of confusion and pain. I hardly spoke except to ask vainly that the music be turned down, or the lights dimmed.

'I'm sorry, Max,' the nurses would say regretfully. 'You'll feel better soon.'

On the second day, they cut my hair.

'We can't wash it while the tongs are in, you see,' a kind voice explained. 'It'll be more comfortable a bit shorter.'

I heard the snip of the scissors three, may be four times, but it didn't seem to make much difference. My scalp still itched terribly as if ants were running through it.

Only with the familiar, loved faces of Sue or Mum beside me did I feel remotely secure. Without them, everything was harder to bear. The wheelchairs seemed to career into my bed more often, the traction weights pulled more relentlessly, and the bustling activity of the ward drained all my resistance. I began to have vivid dreams of running away. I'd jump out of bed and race through the endless corridors to the blessed countryside beyond. Running, running until the ambulance caught up with me and transported my paralysed body back to the ward.

The nights were the worst somehow – long, lonely and empty. Even though the radios were off and voices hushed, all the little night sounds were loud in the darkness. The restlessness of men in pain, a dry cough now and again, the disturbed mumblings of someone dreaming. And sometimes there would be a piercing shout of distress, sending the night nurse running down the ward and shocking me awake. What horror was that nameless patient experiencing? I could never close my eyes again until I'd heard the nurse walk back past the end of my bed.

Every night, my hands were trussed up in splints and bandages to keep my fingers from contracting irrevocably into tight fists. The effect was very strange, as if I was wearing boxing gloves several sizes too large. The hardest part was having the bandages taken off the next morning. My hands always emerged looking thinner than I remembered, with no more colour in them than the bandages themselves. I almost wished they could stay hidden, so I wouldn't have to see how wasted they'd become.

The ward swung into action with gusto at what always seemed an unearthly hour in the mornings. There was no escaping the deftly-wielded flannels, fast-spooned breakfast, linen change and bed bath – all before nine o'clock. To my horror, I discovered that the lifting process was repeated every day in order for the sheets to be smoothed or changed and the pillows shaken. The embarrassment I felt at having an all-over wash, or my urine bag changed, or a suppository prescribed, paled into insignificance beside this reckless dizzy hoist into the air. The orderlies would clutch me to their chests while I doubted I'd ever see solid ground again.

The lifting wasn't my only dread each morning. As soon as the lights went up, I steeled myself for the shivering muscle spasm that shot involuntarily up and down my right side whenever the bed covers were pulled back. It was as if a tiny mechanism was set off somewhere beneath my skin, making half of me tremble and jump like a fish suddenly deprived of water.

No one ever seemed alarmed. Spasticity was apparently a common occurrence after spinal injury. But I was unnerved and embarrassed every time, helpless to control my otherwise lifeless body.

My physiotherapy began again at once, and for a while seemed no more than an extension of the bewildering early-morning activity. It was some time before I actually managed to hold a conversation with the girl who was busily pulling and stretching my limbs.

'My name's Olwyn,' she replied to my question. 'But everyone calls me Ollie.' I realised she must have introduced herself before, but nothing had registered. Shyly, she offered a few more bits of information about herself, and I learnt she came from Newcastle.

'Really?' I exclaimed. 'I was at University there.'

'You were?' She was obviously pleased to have someone to talk to about her home town, and we compared notes for several minutes. It was the first contact I'd really made with anyone on the busy Stoke Mandeville staff.

There were about twenty patients in 2X, each at a different stage of physical progess. Apparently, those at the far end of the ward were closest to being discharged, only a few feet from the French doors leading outside to freedom. Most of the noise that jangled round my head came from that end, although it seemed like I was right in the middle of it.

The occupants of the beds near to me were prostrate and silent. Because they didn't force my attention like the radio music or bright lights, I hardly noticed them at first. It was when I was lying tipped towards my single neighbour one day that I saw he was lying on his stomach, reading. The spectacle took me by surprise. I'd expected him to be on his back like me, but there he was propping himself up on his elbows.

'Perhaps I'll be able to do that soon,' I said to Sue. She told me the boy's name was Gulzar, and that he had some spinal disease which affected the lower half of his body. As I watched him, he moved his shoulders restlessly from side to side. I wondered how long he'd been at Stoke.

'I'm told two and a half years,' Sue replied hesitantly. Two and half years! I didn't dare wonder how long I might stay.

No one ever mentioned the possibility of recovery. No

false hopes were raised, no illusions created. But there were goals to achieve nonetheless.

'Try moving that left hand now,' Ollie would insist after she'd exhausted herself loosening my paralysed muscles. 'And what about your legs?' With Ollie's encouragement, I began to put my mind to making the necessary efforts once more.

It must have been about a week after I'd arrived that I moved my thumb. I spotted it during one of my physio sessions as Ollie was instructing me to try and bend my fingers. I'd been concentrating so hard, willing my fingers to bend, that I thought I'd imagined the tiny movement. Blinking several times, I looked again.

'Hey Ollie,' I was in no doubt now. 'Look at my thumb, my left thumb. It's moving.'

Ollie gave a professional glance at my feebly-moving thumb and a smile crept to her face.

'That's very good, Max,' she said simply.

Ollie was never one to give anything away. She was consistently calm and encouraging whatever progress her patients were making, careful not to betray excitement in case we built up too many hopes.

'It's great isn't it?' I urged, longing for her to make some comment.

'Oh it is,' she nodded. 'Incomplete lesion.'

That took me by surprise. 'What?'

'It means your spinal cord isn't completely severed. If it was you wouldn't be able to move your fingers at all. Someone with a complete lesion can only ever hope to regain movement in his arms and wrists.'

She paused and I drew my own conclusion. 'You mean . . . there's more hope for further movement now?'

'Yes,' in the same casual, smiling tone.

And as if that wasn't encouragement enough, the next day I moved my forefinger – and the next my middle finger. When the tea came round on the fourth day I didn't need Susie's help to eat my biscuit. I could pick it up myself and put it in my mouth. We were euphoric.

By then, pins and needles were shooting down my legs, and I wondered if I dare hope they would regain some movement too.

'Keep trying,' was all Ollie would say as she bent and pulled my aching limbs.

Ollie wasn't the only physiotherapist I got to know during those early days at Stoke Mandeville. Around tea time one afternoon, as my tea sat getting cold beside me, a cheerful voice called from the end of my bed.

'Would you like me to give you your tea?'

Surprised, I met the steady, smiling gaze of a girl I hadn't seen before. Her face was framed by soft dark hair, curling neatly to her shoulders, and she wore a blue-edged uniform like Ollie's.

'Thank you,' I said as she picked up the cup and held the bent straw to my mouth. Usually, if Sue wasn't there, I had to wait for one of the nurses or orderlies to help me, and invariably the tea would be too hot or too cold at the moment of drinking. Unless someone stood over it and judged the temperature, it was impossible to get the timing right.

On this occasion, the tea was warm and refreshing. I swallowed it gratefully.

'I thought I'd pop over and introduce myself,' said my new visitor. 'I know a little bit about Hildenborough Hall and was interested to meet you.'

I was delighted. 'Well, how do you do?'

'My name's Penny. I'm a physio. You probably recognise the uniform.' Her voice had a clipped, open-vowelled character which I tried to place.

'You sound Australian.'

That's right,' Penny grinned, exaggerating her accent as she pronounced the words. She put the empty cup back on my locker.

'We have a small Christian group here that meets every week. You must come along when you're feeling better.'

'That's great, I'd love that.' I spoke from the heart. To think of there being a group of Christians here! I wasn't so isolated after all.

'Anyway, I'll be over for a chat now and again,' continued Penny, adding with a mischievous twinkle, 'Is Ollie working you hard enough?'

'She certainly is.' I was emphatic.

Penny laughed. 'They call us professional bullies, you know.'

The description delighted me. 'Very apt.'

Penny turned to go. 'See you later,' she said, and I returned her cheerful grin.

My spirits lifted beyond measure. For the first time I felt really welcome at Stoke Mandeville. Here was one person at least to whom I could relate on a familiar level. Settling down in this alien place was gradually becoming less of a remote possibility.

I still slept at every quiet opportunity. Now and again, my afternoon dozes were interrupted by the arrival of a visitor, as on the day after I'd met Penny. The rapid approach of high-heeled footsteps intruded into my dreams, followed by muffled exclamations of greeting. I opened my eyes to see Sue and a figure I recognised from Hildenborough disengage themselves from a warm embrace.

'Max, how are you?' the exuberant, ringing voice of Emma called over to me.

'Fine, fine.' Somehow, Emma's cheerfulness always evoked in us a response of similar brightness, whatever we might be feeling underneath.

'You don't look too bad,' Emma said, pulling up a chair beside Sue's. She sat down, unbuttoning her coat but not taking it off.

'I've only called by for a minute. I know how tiring it can be to have visitors chatting on for ages.' She leaned forward eagerly. 'I hear movement is coming back already.'

As a nurse, Emma was interested to hear the specifics of my small recovery, and watched appreciatively as I gave her a demonstration.

'Why that's marvellous.' She sat back admiringly. 'You know, Max, I'm sure you're going to recover completely.'

I was taken aback. Recover completely? Sue and I were

80

taking a day at a time, without expecting too much. Each change for the better was a great bonus – like being given a present. We enjoyed it for what it was, without thinking of what might follow.

Emma obviously thought differently, but her confidence was hard to take. How could she know? I didn't want to start hoping and then be disappointed.

'Well, er . . .' I stumbled for a response, not wanting to hurt Emma's feelings. 'Thank you. . .'

She interrupted gently. 'I've been praying and I know God will heal you.'

I'd recovered myself by then and managed a neutral sentence or two. Emma turned to Sue and asked after the children. The subject was mercifully closed.

A few minutes after Emma had left, Sue started forward in her chair, eyes wide.

'Max,' she whispered. 'I'm sure I saw your foot move.' She pulled back the sheet at the bottom of the bed.

'Try wiggling your toes or something.'

Bemused, I did as I was told, not bothering to ask which foot she meant. I concentrated on moving them both.

'Oh Max. If only you could see. Your toes are moving – on your left foot.' Susie was laughing as if she couldn't quite believe what she saw. 'And just when Emma said you were going to get better.'

It was funny that my toes should have woken up just then, almost as if God was giving me a nudge, hinting that Emma might be proved right.

Emma wasn't the only one praying for us. Letters were pouring in: 'We are sure you will be able to pull through with God's help' . . . 'Just remember we are all behind you' . . . 'Lovely to hear of continued progress. Still praying on.'

Others, like Emma, simply said they were sure God would bring healing. One letter in particular made quite an impression on us:

'This is just a note to assure you of my prayers. I thought you might like to hear of a young friend of mine, Paul, who broke his neck last November and was expecting never to walk again. There was just the tiniest bit of feeling in his toe. Friends all over the world joined in prayer for him, and two months ago he walked from the car to my home for my birthday party. We are all convinced the Lord has used, and will continue to use, the accident to His glory, and I'm sure the same will be true for you.'

We couldn't help but be challenged. Should we be praying for healing? We hadn't thought to do so, feeling God so in control we were content to trust Him rather than ask Him for anything. But perhaps He wanted us to ask too.

A faith-healer? We didn't know anything about them, and as we flipped through the Bible we couldn't find any reference that suggested we should call one. Then Susie remembered the verses she'd read on the evening of the accident. They were in 'Daily Light', a collection of Scripture verses which we used to read every day. There was a theme for each morning and evening, and the theme for the evening of July 23rd had been prayer. James chapter 5, verse 14 onwards had been one of the references.

'Is any among you sick? Let him call for the elders of the church and let them pray over him, anointing him with oil in the name of the Lord, and the prayer of faith will save the sick man and the Lord will raise him up and if he has committed sins he will be forgiven. Therefore, confess your sins to one another and pray for one another, that you may be healed. The prayer of a righteous man has great power in its effects.'

There it was. Something God told His people to do if they were ill. Call the elders of the church to pray. And that had been God's message to us on the very day of the accident, through 'Daily Light'.

'Well, let's do it,' Sue said simply.

'Even the oil?' I wailed. I could happily envisage people praying round me, but the oil was a different matter. It didn't seem very relevant, and it was bound to get all over the sheets and raise a few eyebrows in the hospital.

'The oil's part of the whole thing,' Sue pointed out. 'We shouldn't ignore that if we're taking the rest seriously.' So I was to be anointed as well as prayed over.

'What an excellent idea,' Justyn enthused on his next visit when he heard what we'd decided, and immediately began to think what we could do as well. 'We could have a prayer service in the Chapel at the Hall at the same time. Marvellous opportunity to get lots of people together, and give you specific prayer support.' It was just like J. to come up with something like that. Ideas buzzed through his head at a rate of knots, and our teamwork often consisted of my throwing out the ones that were completely hair-brained and hanging on to the gems. This was a gem.

Poor J. I did feel for him as he sat beside my hospital bed making plans for the day of prayer. 'I'll send out a prayer letter too, so that folk can pray even if they can't make it to the Chapel.' If anyone needed me to be healed, it was J. Running the Hall single-handed again, deciding on his own which ideas to keep and try putting into action. It couldn't be easy. But not a word was said about that. He was as cheerful and encouraging as I'd always known him to be.

So plans steamed ahead for our little anointing service. The next problem was to decide who were our 'elders'.

We belonged to St. Nicholas' Church in Sevenoaks, but our involvement with God's family was as much at the Hall as at the church.

'We ought to think of people who are connected with them both,' I said. Sue sat beside me with pencil poised and address book at the ready.

'One of them must be Justyn.' That was obvious. 'And there's Marcus Collins and James Jones.' They were lay readers at St. Nick's. Both had a gifted teaching ministry, and had spoken at the Hall in the past. I regarded them as men of authority, people I would turn to when I needed help. Should we have anyone else?

'Edward Smith?' suggested Sue. Yes, of course. One of

the folk we'd known longest and a real 'spiritual giant' in our eyes. His support would be invaluable.

The date was set: August 17th. I looked forward to it with a mixture of excitement and apprehension. Would God perform a miraculous healing?

I knew He could, but we were still subject to His will and perhaps He had other plans for me than physical healing. Being physically whole was never what God promised His people as a matter of course. Spiritual wholeness was much more His concern. And he knew what was best for me anyway. Better than I did. I remembered a comment of C. S. Lewis, 'If God had answered all the silly prayers I have prayed in my time, where would I be now?'

If God was going to heal me, that was fine. But if He wasn't, that was fine too.

'He's already healing me anyway,' I said to Sue, moving my arms and hands in demonstration.

We weren't prepared for the setback in store. It happened so quickly, so unexpectedly. One moment I was making progress, and the next I was cast back to the thin divide between life and death.

I couldn't understand what was happening when I woke up that night and felt the ton weight on my chest. It tied me so tightly down I couldn't breathe. Perhaps I should call for the night nurse, but somehow I hesitated to bother her. Even as I decided not to shout, my breath locked in my throat so I couldn't have uttered a sound.

'Max, are you all right?' The voice I'd come to know as belonging to Tommy across the ward called urgently throught the darkness. Since the only reply he got was a muffled gasp and splutter, he employed the emergency yell for me.

'Nurse, nurse. Something's up with Max.'

I still felt stupidly apologetic as the running feet of the nurse approached my bed. Lights went on, faces and voices merged around me, and I sank into unconsciousness, relieved that everyone seemed to know what to do.

For three days it seemed I would never emerge from the

wilderness I'd slipped into. On a drip, all visitors banned and even Susie's face a blur in the greyness, I lay with all the life crushed out of me. I couldn't even draw comfort from knowing God was near, because my mind was too dull to register anything.

That was when God gave Susie a dream. Susie, who'd known from the start that I might not live, who'd watched me improve and drawn hope from it, who'd borne one blow when the journey to Stoke Mandeville set me back and now had to face a second. How devastating it must have been for her to come in as usual that morning and find doctors and nurses surrounding my bed, employing all kinds of equipment to try and keep me alive.

This time it was too much. Stunned and ready to cry, she rushed out of the hospital and back to the car. As she clutched the wheel tightly, she reached out to God in a desperate prayer. Almost at once, peacefulness overtook her desire to cry, and she managed to drive quite calmly back to the hostel. God was already ministering to her in a wonderful way. She never usually slept during the day, but this morning, when she got back to her room, she fell asleep as she lay back on her bed to rest.

As clearly as if she'd been awake and at home looking out over Happy Valley, she saw the sloping green hills and the well-trodden path of many a long walk. Light was pouring in from the far end of the valley, bathing everything in a rich gold. It wasn't like daylight – much warmer and brighter than anything she'd seen before. And sauntering along the path towards the brightness were two figures, their shadows stretching long behind them. She recognised my own tall frame, and the solid one of 'Grandpa' who'd died just a few months previously.

She knew instinctively that this was a picture of heaven. No hurt or suffering spoiled the beauty of the scene, and the light was the light of God.

Curiously enough, her first reaction wasn't to think that I had already crossed the boundary between life and death. Instead she was transfixed by the peace and quiet joy that emanated from the valley. The thought that this was where all God's people were headed thrilled her so deeply that her earlier distress was forgotten. She didn't have to fear for me. What could be more wonderful than being in fellowship with God in eternity?

As she sat beside me during the following long, black days, she was at peace, upheld by the knowledge that I was safe in God's hands.

Our special prayer day drew closer. Were the doctors going to let me have visitors? Slowly, slowly I was finding my way back. Surely I'd be well enough for the service to be conducted as planned.

On the morning of August 17th, Susie opened 'Daily Light' to read as usual. The words jumped from the page to thrill her and confirm that our calling for the elders was in the centre of God's will. 'Pray for one another, that ye may be healed.' I trembled in anticipation as she read the words to me.

'And Max,' she added, looking up from the page. 'I glanced through the rest of the book and the theme of prayer and healing doesn't come anywhere else except on July 23rd, the day of the accident, and today.' It seemed remarkable. What did God have in store?

I was awake and my mind quite clear when our four 'elders' arrived early that afternoon. Miles away at the Hall, people were packed into the Chapel ready to join their prayers with ours, and dotted over the country others were pausing in what they were doing to spend a few moments in prayer. Overseas too, friends and friends of friends were bowing their heads to pray.

My bed was moved into a side ward so our little service could be conducted in privacy and quiet. With my friends grouped soberly around me, and Susie's hand on my shoulder, I just waited peacefully for what God might do.

Justyn began by reading the passage from James, and then, one by one, all four prayed briefly for me. The air was electric as James leant forward to anoint me. He held what seemed a very ordinary bottle of probably very ordinary oil, and as he uncorked it he gave me one of his cheerful, warm-hearted grins, as if he too found this bit of the service rather strange. I felt his touch on my neck, and the moment had come.

Should I try and get out of bed? No. God would make it clear what He wanted me to do. It was up to Him now.

Nothing changed. No lightning struck. I knew I was still paralysed. The faces around my bed waited solemnly, expectantly for a few seconds, and then moved to go. We'd only been given a short time, and it was up. With a quiet 'goodbye', a touch on my shoulder and 'God bless you', each left my bedside.

It was all over so quickly. For a moment I wondered if they'd really been and gone again. But of course they had. The oil was still sticky on my neck. Disappointment nagged at me, even though I'd known God might withold His power.

I stared helplessly at the ceiling.

Yet God couldn't have failed me. I knew deep down that some day His purpose would be revealed and the answers to our prayers made clear. There was no doubt in my mind that we'd done right to have the prayer service. It was a fulfilment of one of God's commands, and on that strength alone was worthwhile. But how hard it was just now to accept that no miracle had resulted.

A long time afterwards, I learnt what a variety of expectations my 'elders' had brought with them. One felt sure that God would heal, but was prepared to accept that it might be over a period of time. A second knew I was safe in God's hands, but subject to His will – which might not be for healing. James was the bearer of a gift from some mutual friends, intended both to comfort and encourage, but at the last minute kept it in his pocket. It was a book about a man who was confined to a wheelchair after a serious illness, yet who testified to God's abundant faithfulness. James found he couldn't give me the book after all: it would have seemed as if they only expected God to get me to a wheelchair.

And Justyn came with a spare seat in his car, to take me home. He was the most bitterly disappointed.

It seemed ages before Sue came back into the side ward after seeing the others off.

'Okay Mac?' She put her hand on my shoulder, and I knew she felt the same mixture of gladness and disappointment as I did.

The next day was very grim. I was still getting used to the new drugs given to counteract the effects of the asthmatic attack. They made me nauseous and dizzy, susceptible all over again to the noisy irritations of 2X. I clung to the knowledge that people were praying, that Susie was with me, that I was alive, despite all, and in the hands of God.

With agonising slowness, I crawled back to firm ground.

It must have been two or three days later that Sue burst in to the ward more excitedly than usual and held a posy of tiny wild flowers over my head.

'Look Mac. Aren't these lovely?' Bright red and yellow vetch peeped through fronds of grasses, together with daisies and soft purple campion. Globes of dandelion too, and more purple flowers I didn't recognise.

'Where did you find those?' I asked, sniffing appreciatively at their delicate scent.

'Just outside.' Sue was breathless and her eyes shone. 'They were growing on a *rubbish dump*!'

'Really?' Susie was capable of finding something pretty in the most obscure places.

'I walk past it every day – it belongs to the hospital, I think. I never noticed all these lovely flowers before though. Who'd have thought a rubbish dump could be anything but ugly and useless.'

She rummaged in her bag and pulled out a jam jar – 'I begged it from the kitchen' – and began to arrange her find.

'They looked so odd, in among the broken bottles and bits of paper,' she chattered on. 'You should have seen how they clung to the tiniest bit of soil. And once I'd spotted them,

88

the rubbish dump seemed transformed – sprinkled all over with colour.'

She finished her arrangement and disappeared for a moment to fill the jar with water.

'There!' She placed the posy of colour on my bedside table where I could see it, and stood back in admiration.

'Lovely,' I said.

Sue pulled up her chair and sat down, elbows on the bed and chin cupped in her hands.

'You know,' she began, more serious now. 'I had an idea while I was looking at those flowers on the rubbish dump.'

'Mmm?' I prompted, for she'd gone quiet, a sign that she had something serious to say and was searching for the right words.

'What's happened to you, to us . . .' Another pause. 'It's like the rubbish dump in a way. I mean. . .' She frowned, as if the words had already come out wrongly. 'I mean, your suffering and paralysis seem awful, pointless, a waste of your life. Yet we don't know what God might do with our life as it is now. To Him it isn't a waste. If He can bring flowers from a heap of rubbish, what might He bring out of our situation?'

She took a deep breath, and looked at me questioningly to see if I'd understood what she'd been trying to say. I could see the picture she had in her mind, but couldn't immediately apply it to myself. The silence grew long, and I tried to relieve it with some response.

'You mean God doesn't always take away things that are difficult, painful, but transforms them – brings something else from them, like the flowers.'

'Something beautiful,' Sue added emphatically, as if I'd missed the most important point of her words.

'Yes.' I saw it suddenly in a flash of recognition. So simple. I looked again at the flowers, bright and pretty in their jar. A new optimism welled up inside me.

'Well,' I said to Susie, a tremble of excitement in my voice. 'I wonder what flowers He'll grow on our "rubbish dump"?'

# CHAPTER 6

It was tea time during a quiet afternoon. I'd slept for a couple of hours, undisturbed by visitors who were still being asked to stay away while I recovered from the asthmatic attack.

The others were back from their afternoon session of Occupational Therapy, and I could hear them exchanging jokes across the table at the far end of the ward. I tried to picture them all in their wheelchairs, holding their cups for themselves and leisurely drinking. Tea didn't taste the same out of a straw.

Susie was tipping the cup for me to trap the last mouthful when brisk footsteps and the swish of a starched uniform announced the arrival of Sister Clements. I was surprised to see her. Normally she'd be taking her own tea break about now.

'Max, we're going to move you up the ward,' she announced even more surprisingly. This wasn't the usual time for any rearrangement of beds.

Before I could ask what was going on, Sister Clements had released the brake at the head of my bed and was calling 'Ready?' to someone down at the other end. Her face wore its most serious, efficient expression. Her youthful features were drawn into tight seriousness, belying the good humour and kindness that lay underneath.

'Okay,' she called to her helper. The brake was flipped on again and I was left staring at the entrance doors to the ward. Behind me, others were being moved too, and after a couple of minutes my bed was pushed back against the wall. I was only one place along from where I'd been before.

Perhaps this was my first promotion. The doctors considered me well enough to climb one rung of the ladder towards ultimate release.

'I'm making progress then, am I?' I called to Sister Clements as I heard her rush by again.

'Someone else needs the corner position,' came the reply. And then, as if realising she hadn't quite answered my question, she added, 'But yes, you're making progress too.'

At last I realised what was happening. A new 'emergency case' was being admitted. There must have been all this activity when I first came.

Over in the corner, a new bed was being made up, several nurses working to get it prepared quickly.

'It's a racing driver,' Sue told me after speaking briefly with one of the busy staff. 'He's coming straight from Silverstone. And it's his neck that's broken rather than his back.' I looked soberly towards the empty bed. If it was his neck, he would probably be completely paralysed, at least to begin with. A back break left normal movement in the top half of the body.

Voices and more hurried steps grew closer, and the clatter of a wheeled stretcher. A little knot of doctors and nurses appeared, surrounding the still figure of the racing driver, and Sister Clements organised the lifting team almost immediately. As I watched the newcomer being moved, I wondered if he was as frightened as I had been. I didn't hear him cry out.

He was still in his asbestos suit. It seemed that part of it was going to have to be cut if he was to be freed from it. I thought of my shirt, folded and forgotten now. But this young man was under no illusions about being allowed home shortly.

'Put a label on it,' he instructed the nurse who was taking off the suit, 'and send it back to the stewards. It's too valuable to waste, and I won't be needing it again.'

I was stunned by the calmness of his voice. He knew his racing days were over, and seemed already to have accepted it. I suppose he'd been aware at the start of every race that he was taking a risk, so perhaps he'd in some measure prepared himself. I couldn't tell how he was feeling now that the risk had proved almost fatal, but I knew that if my accident had been the result of such consciously-wooed danger, I couldn't have forgiven myself. It was bad enough

91

facing the consequences. Self-accusation too would have been unbearable.

'Oh Max,' Sue whispered sorrowfully a little while later. 'Here are his parents. They look terribly upset.' I couldn't see them as I was turned to face the ceiling again, but I could imagine their distress.

'The hospital will be so confusing for them too,' continued Sue. 'I must tell them what happens and where things are.' That was probably the only way we could be of any help.

I could hear the family talking quietly. 'At least he's conscious,' I remarked, and Susie nodded. A chair scraped, and Sue got up in her turn.

'It's his mother. I'll just pop over and speak to her.'

I listened to the soft exchange of voices, the one concerned and the other hesitantly grateful.

'This is my husband, Max. Mrs. Alexander.' A fair-haired, attractive woman stood beside Sue, her face tense and sparkles of tears in her eyes.

'I'm sorry you too . . .' she said, but couldn't finish the sentence.

I so much wanted to comfort her by assuring her of God's care even in such tragedy, but feared that it would sound too glib just then. It was Sue who eventually shared what we believed.

'We've found it an immense help to know that God must have a plan in this somewhere.' The words came out so naturally and simply, they evoked a thoughtful nod from Mrs. Alexander.

'I . . . I don't quite have the faith to say that, but I'm sure you're right.'

Perhaps it was my imagination, but after that she seemed more at peace when she came over for a chat, as if deep down a buried faith had been awakened. I remembered the prayer Susie and I had said when we first arrived at Stoke – simply, 'Lord, use us here.' We knew only He could provide the openings.

Surprisingly enough, the racing driver was awake when I was turned towards him again the next day. With stiff, awkward hands he was agitating the sheet that covered him as if it was rough on his skin. I was amazed he could move at all.

He was the one to introduce himself – Dave Alexander. I'd hesitated to speak in case he was feeling too ill to respond, but he was actually quite alert.

'They tell me I've escaped spinal shock,' he told me informatively when I commented on his hand movement. 'So everything's functioning. Don't quite know why, but I'm certainly glad. I was lucky not to have any head injuries, so don't feel too bad in myself.'

I didn't like to ask him then about his accident, but he volunteered the story himself as if he needed to get it out of his system.

'Stupid really,' he began. His tone was matter-of-fact, without bitterness. 'Everything was fine until this chap cut in front of me. I had to swerve out of his way and ended up crashing at 100 miles an hour into one of the safety barriers – backwards that is. 'Spose my neck just cracked with the force of the impact.'

'Was anyone else involved?' I asked tentatively.

'Oh no. I went off the track you see. I think they finished the race and everything. When you're racing you don't always notice if someone's gone off the track. You just keep going. I don't suppose they knew there'd been an accident until the end.'

'Well,' I tried to think of some comfort. 'If your hands aren't paralysed, at least you won't have to wear boxing gloves.' His reaction was predictably puzzled.

'What do you mean, boxing gloves?'

I explained.

'Oh, that's too bad,' came the sympathetic reply. 'Will you always have to wear them?'

'I don't know.'

I hadn't asked anyone. It was another of those things I accepted as necessary without dwelling too much on the implications. I hadn't thought far enough ahead to wonder how long I'd have to put up with them. For a moment I saw myself at home with Susie trussing up my hands every night. . .

'What happened to you then?' Dave continued the conversation and interrupted my gloomy thoughts.

Briefly, I told him about that early July morning and the orange Capri.

'Whew,' Dave whistled softly through his teeth. 'Wrong way round really, you being hurt and the other driver escaping with barely a scratch.'

'It would have been worse if we'd both ended up in hospital.'

It was strange how little I'd thought back to the driver of the Capri. Certainly, I felt no resentment towards him. He was just a vague figure in my memory, grey-faced and shaken, sipping from his steaming cup. He hadn't been to visit me, and as I thought about it I wasn't surprised and didn't really mind. Perhaps it was better that we each reconciled ourselves in our own way to what had happened.

'I expect it's as hard to live with the thought of what you've done to someone else as it is to cope with the injuries themselves,' I said to Dave.

I didn't appreciate then how much God was protecting me from the cancer of bitterness. Later I did feel resentful, and couldn't find the way back to forgive without God's help.

\*    \*    \*    \*    \*    \*

Before Dave arrived I'd barely spoken to my fellow-patients. Tommy Barrett, who'd raised the alarm the night of my asthmatic attack, was the only one I'd made any contact with. He was in the opposite bed, having been admitted the same day as I was. I learnt from Susie that he was the one who'd stolen my helicopter! Plucking up courage after talking to Dave, I made my first attempt at cross-ward conversation.

'Hello Tommy. I'm Max.' I wondered if he could hear me over the noise of the television. Since my chest muscles were paralysed I couldn't shout very loud.

'Hi Max,' came the friendly, thin-voiced reply. 'Nice to hear you.'

I was suddenly stuck for words. In preparing what I might say, I hadn't got past the method of introduction. Then I remembered the helicopter.

'Hear you came in the helicopter that was supposed to fly me.'

'Yeah.' He sounded apologetic. 'Suppose they gave priority to one of their own. Navy helicopter, y'see, and I was stationed on the Ark Royal.'

It was strange to be having a conversation with someone I couldn't see. It was like being blind, trying to imagine a face to fit the voice.

'Hey, what do you look like?' The question was his. He must be finding it equally strange not to be able to see me. I experimented with 'tall, dark and handsome', but Tommy seemed more inclined to believe the 'fair, ginger-haired' version. He, apparently, was *small*, dark and handsome!

'And, how are you feeling?' The words were more tentative.

'Better than I was. My appetite's coming back, which is always a good sign.'

'Mine too.' Tommy sounded pleased to find something we had in common. 'And what about movement? Can you do much?'

There was more at stake here somehow. I knew Tommy's neck break was similar to mine, and was as curious as he was to find out whether our physical progress was the same. Yet suppose he was 'further on' than me?

'Well,' I answered hesitantly, aware that Tommy might be disappointed too. 'I can move my arms and hands a little. And the toes on one foot.'

'Both my arms are fine, and my hands seem to be okay. But nothing in my legs.'

There was a pause. Who were we to tell what recovery at this stage meant for the future? So I reasoned with myself, but couldn't help feeling cast down that Tommy had the use

95

of his hands while mine were all but paralysed. Probably he felt the same about the movement in my foot.

'Tell me when your hands improve,' he said.

'And you your legs.'

We kept tabs on each other after that. It was a surprising relief just to share things with someone in a similar predicament.

Gradually, I got to know others too. Sue and Mum were instrumental in breaking the ice at first, going down the ward and chatting to the patients and then telling me something about them.

'Who's the one with the loud voice?' I asked Sue after one of her little excursions. It was impossible not to notice the succession of complaints and exaggerated groans of pain coming from the other side of the ward.

'Ah, that's Rasputin,' replied Susie in a stage whisper. 'At least, that's what I've nicknamed him. He's called Dave Pembury really, but he's got this amazing beard that's growing everywhere and makes him look like Rasputin.' From then on, a vivid image of a prostrate Rasputin was conjured up in my mind every time I heard Dave Pembury's Cockney voice.

One morning he surprised us all. It was still fairly early, with breakfast just being brought round and the sleep barely washed out of our eyes, when his familiar tones struck up much more cheerfully than usual. I could hardly believe my ears. He was telling jokes to the orderlies – Irish ones at that. One after another they rolled out, doubling up his listeners and gradually affecting us all.

'Have you heard the one about the Irish man who never went water ski-ing because he couldn't find any sloping water?' That's when the laughter caught me. It was the first time I'd really laughed since the accident. The whole ward rippled with little explosions of appreciation as Dave drew out joke after joke from his seemingly never-ending store.

With Dave Alexander's arrival in the corner, I now found myself next to the Cockney joker. I knew it must be him,

96

because Sue's Rasputin description fitted my new neighbour perfectly.

We were turned towards each other at the same time.

'Hello,' I began with some trepidation. Before I spoke to Tommy I already felt a certain bond with him because of our similar circumstances, but I wasn't sure of any common ground with Dave.

''ello,' he returned gruffly. His broad arms lay outside the sheets, and a huge tattoo caught my eye on one of them. As I looked, he brought one hand up to loosen the bedclothes across his chest.

'So you can move your arms then,' I said almost without thinking.

'Low back break,' Rasputin answered. 'Legs are as dead as doornails though.'

'Ah.'

'How long 'ave you been 'ere then?' Rasputin gallantly opened up a new avenue for the conversation. We established that I'd arrived first by about two days.

''ang on a minute. Is it your missis who's come and said 'ello every now and then these last few days?'

'Probably. She's with the folks of the racing driver just now.'

'Sue isn't it? And you're Max.' Rasputin was looking at me a little less suspiciously now.

'That's right.'

'Chartered Accountant, I hear.' Sue must have had quite a long conversation with him. 'Not my world at all, that.' I wasn't sure how to respond to the note of antagonism I heard in his voice.

'What is your world?' I asked after a pause.

'Oh, cars is mine. Second hand car dealer. Had me accident driving back from an auction. A Mini it was.'

'Mine was a car accident too.' It occurred to me that Dave might be interested to hear about our Plymouth Baracuda, so I mentioned how it had really saved us from any worse injury because it was so strongly built.

'Good solid cars them,' Dave agreed approvingly.

97

Once again, there was silence.

'Glad to hear you're pulling out of that asthmatic attack,' was Dave's next, surprising comment. His concern warmed me to him at once.

'Those jokes of yours helped,' I grinned. He chuckled from deep in his chest, and then cleared his throat.

'I think I've got one here you won't have heard . . .'

Suddenly there was a link between us. It was just there, despite all the obvious differences in our characters. Our common ground was our common situation. I laughed uproariously at the new joke.

I was beginning to feel better, well enough to receive visitors again. The ban was lifted, and I looked eagerly for the first face to appear round the corner of my bed.

I couldn't quite place him at first. A good-looking young man with a shy smile. Then I remembered. Robert Todd. He and his family were regular visitors at Hildenborough.

'Hello Max,' he said, depositing a huge basket of fruit on my locker. 'That's from my parents really. They send their greetings.'

Through his rather formal manner, I could sense that Robert felt uneasy in the hospital. He darted furtive looks about him as he explained how he and his brother Timmy were passing through and thought they'd stop by. Timmy grinned at me from his brother's side. He seemed more relaxed, although he looked doubtfully at all the paraphernalia surrounding my head.

'Well it's very good of you to come,' I said as cheerfully as I could, hoping to put the boys at ease. 'Do you know you are my first visitors for almost a week? You're lucky the doctors let you in.'

Robert laughed politely, and then asked several carefully phrased questions as to how I was feeling. I wished I could distract him from his obvious discomfort. He wasn't the first to be taken aback by my gruesome appearance and the whole atmosphere of the hospital. Several times I'd found myself cheering up my visitors instead of the other way round.

'Tell me what you're doing now,' I enquired as the conversation flagged a little. 'Any new projects on hand?'

'Well, yes, as a matter of fact.' Robert leant forward eagerly and told me he'd decided to become a racing driver. 'I haven't really squared it with my parents, but we're going to talk about it again when we've all given it more thought.'

I couldn't help but think of Dave Alexander next door. Before I'd realised what effect my words might have on poor Robert, I'd blurted out, 'That's interesting. The chap in the corner there is – er, *was* a racing driver. And I think there's another one further up the ward.'

Robert, already white, went whiter still. Suddenly, his eyes turned skyward and he disappeared from view. There was a resounding crash and clatter of chairs.

Timmy and I looked blankly at each other.

'Where's Robert?' I asked rather stupidly. Timmy looked down at the floor, then back at me, and down at the floor again.

'He's fainted,' he said incredulously. 'He's just fainted.'

I had to be more careful about what I said to cheer my visitors up after that.

In the evenings, the general hubbub in the ward reached its loudest pitch. Physio and occupational therapy were complete for the day, and lengthy post mortems were indulged in across the ward. Visitors came to and fro, and radios and cassette recorders were played at full blast. More often than not, ten o'clock found me with a blinding headache and longing for the comparative peace of the night.

'How about trying some television?' Susie suggested one evening when the cacophony of noise around us seemed even worse than usual.

'Television?' Sue knew how much I hated the continually blaring set at the far end of the ward. 'I couldn't see that one even if I wanted to.'

'No – I mean I could get you a little portable one to watch right here. It's the Rockford Files tonight.'

My attitude changed at once. Rockford was my favourite American private investigator.

'Oh yes,' I cried, eager now. 'What a great idea.' The thought of watching the programme I'd enjoyed for years brought a refreshing gust of the outside world into 2X. 'But where did you find a portable television?'

Susie grinned at me over her shoulder as she headed for the doors.

'I spotted it in the next ward yesterday. They said I could borrow it.'

A few minutes later, the set was perched on my locker.

'Here goes,' Sue said cheerfully, and switched on. Tipped up on my side, and with a good, if slanted, view of the screen, I looked forward to fifty minutes of welcome distraction.

After barely ten, however, my head was spinning with the effort of concentration. I couldn't understand why I was finding it such a strain just to watch television. I'd been feeling better, so what was wrong? I tried to enjoy the programme, but waves of nausea began to wash over me until finally I had to admit defeat.

'It's no good.' Disappointment rang through my voice. 'I can't concentrate. Next time perhaps.' It seemed unbelievable that I couldn't even manage to watch television. I couldn't be much better after all. My new optimism was rudely dashed to the ground.

Obviously the doctors thought I was making good progress nonetheless because a few days later, towards the end of August, they told Susie she could go home if she wished. I was out of danger.

'That's wonderful, isn't it, Max?' Susie said gratefully after she'd heard the news. 'All those prayers – they were answered.'

'Yes,' I acknowledged, but inside I was feeling panicky at the thought of Susie leaving me. I couldn't really take in the significance of the doctors' assurances as I tried to imagine what Stoke Mandeville would be like without Sue to talk to, to give me my tea and meals, to make contact with the other patients.

The engulfing loneliness I'd felt when my two friends from Exeter left me at the beginning swept over me again.

'I wish you didn't have to go,' I said in a small voice.

'I'll come back as often as I can – every weekend. And you can look forward to the children coming to see you when the traction is off.'

But that seemed such a long way ahead. If all went well, it would be three weeks – almost as long as I'd already spent in hospital.

Noddy's last letter was pinned up on the wall behind my bed. 'We're looking forward to coming to see you soon.' Sue and I had agreed that they shouldn't visit before the traction was off. Seeing me stuck in bed on my back would be enough for them to face without the horror of the traction as well. And it was a horror by now. Quite apart from the machinery itself, my unwashed hair looked dreadful. Flaking dandruff everywhere, despite the oil that was rubbed in to moisten my scalp. I longed for my first hair wash almost as much as release from the traction: to be rid of the unbearable itching . . .

'I'll buy you a new tape cassette to celebrate,' Susie was saying.

'Celebrate your going?' The moody words escaped me before I could stop them.

'Celebrate your getting better – and to help pass the time.'

Justyn on his last visit had thoughtfully provided a cassette player which I'd just begun to enjoy. I'd discovered I could shut out the noise of the ward with the headphones.

'Sounds a good idea,' I said, trying to sound appreciative of Sue's thoughtful suggestion.

Sue found the latest recording of Jamie Owens, one of my favourite singers.

'You can't fail to like this,' she told me as she slotted it into the cassette player just before she left. She popped the snug-fitting headphones over my ears and gave me a quick kiss of farewell.

'Goodbye,' I saw her mouth say. 'See you next weekend,' and she was gone.

The tape whirred and wound its way to the first guitar chords. Their familiarity was soothing. I knew all Jamie's music, and though I hadn't heard this album before, the distinctive style I'd always loved was the same as ever. The clear, sweet voice, thoughtful words, gentle music. I closed my eyes and imagined Jamie right beside my bed, singing as she had done at the Hall barely two years before.

But there was something different about these lyrics. Jamie was singing about conflict. inner turmoil, suffering. As one song succeeded another, I identified more and more with the emotions expressed. The words might have been mine.

> I've done all I know,
> Gone as far as I can go,
> And I'm praying that You will take me through.
> My strength's all run out
> And I'm almost starting to doubt
> That I can make it
> Oh Lord, it's up to you.

That was my prayer. Once again, I was at the foot of the cross, laying down my burden and seeing it taken up patiently by my Saviour.

> 'Cause I've never had to go this far before.
> And I don't know if I can do it.
> No I've never had to go this far before,
> And I'm countin' on You to see me through it.

> My dreams all lie dead,
> Can't see any light ahead,
> But I'm trustin' You'll carry me along.
> 'Cause I've heard Your voice,
> And my heart has made its choice
> To believe You
> When You say it won't be long.

102

Jamie knew something of what I was going through. She hadn't broken her neck, but had obviously struggled with some equally devastating test of faith. She helped me to feel less isolated. I was struck by the thought that there was a certain universality of experience among Christians facing a crisis. The same sense of devastation and longing for God's help could accompany a domestic or financial problem as well as a broken neck. People faced difficulties of some kind or another every day. Mine was no unique trial. It comforted me to know that, and I listened to the cassette over and over again.

I've gone as far as I can go, Lord, and I'm praying You'll take me through. Oh Lord, it's up to You.

# CHAPTER 7

It was Sue's birthday two days after she left. We hadn't spent a birthday apart since our marriage.

I spent ages trying to devise a way of getting her a card. I always used to make a special trip to the shop, looking carefully through every card before I made my choice. There was no way I could do that now. Someone else would have to go for me. The idea didn't appeal at all. Who could I entrust with such a personal errand?

Of course, Mum would go. Staying to keep me company for a while longer, she would have time to choose something.

'A Susie-type card,' I instructed her. 'One with flowers on perhaps.'

Mum duly found a pretty card that Sue was sure to like,

but unreasonably I still felt I'd have chosen something different. I couldn't reconcile myself to this denial of something I'd done for years.

'What would you like me to say, Max?' Mum asked as she prepared to write inside the card. I thought of all the little things I might put, but again found myself frustrated because I couldn't write them myself.

'Just put love from Max,' I said finally. So the card was sent with nothing more than that.

The week went by slowly until finally Sue's bright smile and 'hello' dismissed Jamie Owens for the weekend.

'I've brought you a piece of cake,' was her first announcement, and she delved into her bag for the napkin-wrapped offering.

'Noddy made it for my birthday.'

'Did she indeed,' I chuckled. 'It looks quite edible.'

'Of course.' Susie's eyebrows went up in instinctive, motherly defence of Noddy's effort. 'It was a surprise. She did it all by herself – I just helped with the oven.'

Thinking of Noddy battling away with the mixing bowl at Pepperland, I felt suddenly nostalgic for home. It seemed so long since I was there, taking Sunny for a walk through Happy Valley. How long would it be before I was back?

'Are the children all right?' I asked vaguely.

'Fine – missing you.'

As if she sensed that home wasn't a cheering subject just then, Susie determinedly got me telling her about all that had happened in 2X since she'd been away. There wasn't much to report, except my experience as a guinea pig. It was common knowledge throughout Stoke Mandeville by now that I was a 'case', that my particular form of semi-paralysis was unusual and therefore of great interest to the medical staff. There was more movement in my left side than my right, but no sensation, whereas I could feel quite a bit now down my right side. I was sort of split in half.

'Most interesting case,' the Consultant had pronounced to his students as they grouped round my bed for the visual aid to their lecture. 'A classic Brown Sequard. We average about two patients a year with this syndrome.' Dr Maynard launched impressively into detailed explanation of my 'syndrome', bending his dark, balding head toward me now and again to demonstrate with a pin or a little hammer what I could feel or move. His shoulders were hunched slightly even when standing up, as if he'd spent a lot of time stooping over patients.

'And notice the eyes too,' continued my Consultant when the first part of his lecture was over. 'This is a good example of the Horner Syndrome, where the pupil of the eye on the side of the body that is paralysed is noticeably larger than the other.'

As the students dutifully scrutinised my eyes, Dr Maynard interrupted his discourse to say kindly to me, 'I hope you don't mind all this, Mr Sinclair. It is so useful for the students.'

'Of course,' I replied, although I was feeling more like an object than a person, summed up so neatly in medical terms.

I was at least beginning to understand a little more about my physical state. When 'C5' was talked about, I didn't wonder what new ward was being referred to but understood that my neck break had occurred at the fifth vertebra of my cervical column. 'Incomplete lesion' I understood, and I felt a tremble of excitement whenever it was mentioned. There was still hope for more, and better movement.

That weekend with Susie was a quiet one. It was our wedding anniversary, and never had we felt less like celebrating. Being stuck in the hospital seemed harder to bear because normally we went out for a meal on our anniversary, a little tradition that had come to mean a lot to us. We rarely treated ourselves to a restaurant meal, and it seemed that the tenth anniversary should have been extra special.

'At least we celebrated with Bob and Rachel,' Sue said stalwartly.

'Mmm.'

'The whole of that week was fun really, wasn't it?'

I thought back. The busy conference week at the Hall,

Annie's birthday party, the unforgettable evening with our old friends in Devon.

'Yes, I suppose it was.'

'It was very good of the Lord to give us such special moments before all this happened,' Sue continued. I felt the same, but somehow the misery of the present loomed larger. There was so much we now had to face.

By the time Sunday arrived, we'd stopped even trying to be cheerful. Our goodbyes lingered.

'Oh Max,' Susie cried suddenly, clapping her hand to her mouth. 'I forgot Annie Tollast's present. Elderflower champagne – we were supposed to have it yesterday for our anniversary. It's still sitting in the fridge at the hostel.'

We might have laughed, but couldn't then. We were only reminded of our despondency which had meant even champagne was forgotten.

Mum left as well that weekend, so I was properly on my own for the first time in five weeks. Many of the long hours were spent listening to my precious cassettes: Dave Pope, Nutshell and of course, Jamie Owens. The only difficulty was I couldn't operate the player myself and had to call one of the busy staff every time I wanted a cassette changed. Since many of the orderlies were foreign, with only a limited command of English, this wasn't always an easy process.

'The Jamie Owens tape, please,' I'd say when one of them answered my call.

A grunt and frown of incomprehension.

'The cassette with the blue markings,' I'd then say, very slowly. 'In my locker.'

If I still wasn't understood, I'd move my hand slowly to the player that lived during the day on my bed and tap it as best I could. That usually worked, and the orderly would then spend several seconds looking wildly round for my store of tapes. Once he'd spotted them in the locker, it was a question of patiently saying 'yes' or 'no' until he found the right one.

A whole new set of problems arose when I simply wanted the cassette changed over. For a start, the headphones

106

blocked out any sound so I couldn't tell if anyone was near to help me. I'd resort to a hearty shout when I'd plucked up the courage, only to find more often than not that a nurse had been round the other side of my bed and didn't take to my deafening roar. If an orderly appeared, I had to make him understand that I *didn't* want a cassette from the locker this time, but a simple changeover. On one occasion, my headphones were taken off and everything carefully put away before my desire was finally communicated.

It was wearying to have to fight so hard to achieve one small thing. Sometimes it didn't seem worth even trying. I was tempted just to lie back and let the hospital day go by in its usual routine way without disturbance from me.

One afternoon I couldn't face calling anyone to turn over my Jamie Owens cassette. The last track on side one had faded several minutes before and I lay listening to silent headphones. Then it occurred to me to try turning the cassette myself. Why not? I had nothing to lose. A fierce determination took hold of me and I reached towards the recorder.

With agonising slowness, I felt for the button to reject the cassette. Ah, that was it. Was it stuck? A bit more effort perhaps. My finger was so weak it couldn't exert the pressure necessary to move the button. Minutes passed, and then at last the tape popped up.

Getting it out wasn't too difficult. I slid my finger underneath and drew back my hand. The tape fell on to the bed, and I fumbled awkwardly for several more minutes trying to turn it over and pick it up again. When at last it was back in my hand, I couldn't find the right position to insert it once more. Every time I pushed it against the little 'drawer' it was supposed to slide into so easily, I met some block.

My arm was aching with the effort, and I wondered if I was going to have to admit defeat and call for help. Then the tape found its slot and slipped into place. I banged down the top, and began the search for the 'on' button. There it was. Just a little more push, and the player lurched into

107

action. I hardly heard the music for the relief and triumph that flooded over me.

It had taken me twenty minutes – but I'd done it.

Next, I learned to take off my headphones by plopping my arms over my head and pulling downwards. The headphones ended up round my neck. Not that I could put them on again – but it was a start. It seemed I was on the way to some small measure of independence after weeks of total reliance on those around me.

It must have been just into September when my soft-voiced, Scottish occupational therapist, Rosemary, came up with a surprising suggestion.

'What about trying some reading?'

She couldn't be serious.

'You must be joking,' I said in amazement. 'I can't even hold a book.'

'Ah, but you won't have to hold it,' came the mysterious response. 'Have you ever heard of a reading stand?'

A reading stand! How could that work with me lying flat on my back?

'It's very simple really,' assured Rosemary, busy setting up a metal cage-like affair around my bed. 'You put the book on the stand like – so,' and she deftly set a little paperback she'd brought with her on the wooden slat which was positioned directly above my head. 'And you turn the pages like – so,' demonstrating with a wooden stick how to flip the pages from under the rubber band that held them in place and tuck them under the corresponding band on the other side.

I tried to follow her example, but failed at every attempt. I couldn't hold the stick properly, and although it was firmly strapped to my hand it took me a long time to wield it to any effect. And when I did manage to move the pages, I turned over about ten at once.

Rosemary was laughing.

'Don't worry. You'll soon get the hang of it.'

'Soon' meant two or three days, but then a whole new world opened up for me in 2X. I lost myself in page after page, and eagerly instructed Sue over the phone to bring all my favourite Nevil Shute and James Herriot from home.

'I've brought you another one too,' she said as she deposited mounds of paperbacks on my locker the following weekend. She waved the book over my head. There was a picture of a smiling girl with short hair on the front, and the title looked like someone's signature.

'What's this?'

'Present! It's about a girl who broke her neck and never regained any movement.'

Sue fixed the book on to my reading stand while I thought I'd rather read something less demanding.

'It's very special,' Sue added, reading my thoughts. 'You won't be able to put it down.'

So I was introduced to Joni, the young American girl named after her father Johnny and insisting in the first few pages of her book that the two names were pronounced the same. From the start I knew I was reading something of the same heartfelt character as Jamie Owens' songs, concerned with a similar struggle and the same eternal truths. But this time, the experiences directly corresponded with mine, from the moment of the diving accident in which Joni broke her neck to the months of frustration in hospital.

Sue was right. I read hungrily from beginning to end, every page moving, challenging or humbling me.

'I really began to see suffering in a new light,' I read. 'Not as trials to avoid, but as opportunuties to "grab" because God gives so much of His love, grace and goodness to those who do.'

I hadn't thought of suffering as a privilege before. Here was someone who'd learnt to see it as something positive, even exciting, a chance for God to enter her life in a much more real way.

So many of her experiences exactly paralleled my own. Joni had been bewildered by the hospital, blinded by its lights and disturbed by its noise. She had alternately laughed and wept, hoped and despaired, been moody and taken those she loved for granted. Her first tiny hand movement had been a triumph like my own, although she wasn't ever to gain much more. She'd had a tougher time than me, and yet still come through it praising God.

It was exhilarating to read of this ultimate victory over suffering, yet I found myself questioning whether Joni had highlighted the positive side of her experience for the benefit of her readers. Did she really feel no resentment or doubt now? I wished I could meet her to find out. Still unsure that I would be able to reconcile myself to being handicapped for the rest of my life, I longed for uncontested reassurance that with Christ I had the means to be totally victorious. I knew it by faith, and Joni's book provided vital encouragement, but it wasn't until later I got the answer to my question.

By the end of the book I felt I knew Joni personally. She became a quiet companion as my stay at Stoke Mandeville lengthened.

After seven and a half weeks, it was time for the traction to come off.

'An X-ray first,' ordered Dr. Maynard. Just in case the bone hasn't healed sufficiently.' I must have looked alarmed, because he added, 'We always do it, Mr. Sinclair. A routine check.'

I was whisked off to the X-ray department, the first time I'd been out of the ward since my arrival. I still couldn't see more than the ceiling, but the bright skylights didn't hurt my eyes any more, and the music and hubbub from the other wards sounded cheerful. The X-ray machinery seemed far less awesome than I remembered, and the 'routine check' was over very quickly.

'Fine, fine,' came Dr. Maynard's welcome voice at last. 'The tongs can come out.'

I wondered how this would be done, what it would feel like, whether I'd be able to move my head straight away afterwards. Surprisingly, I hadn't thought about any of these things before. My preoccupation had always been with the relief I'd feel once the weights were removed.

'We can't just take them out at once, you know,' one of

the nurses warned me. 'We have to take the weights off gradually so you'll have time to get used to the change. The tongs are last.'

That didn't make much sense to me until the first two pounds were taken off. My head seemed to float up and suspend itself dizzily somewhere near the ceiling, and I couldn't focus my eyes properly for several minutes. I was glad when they told me the next couple of pounds wouldn't be coming off for another two hours. That would leave only two more pounds to go. I imagined my head floating away beyond recall and laughed out loud.

When finally all the weights had been removed, Dr. Maynard came over to take the tongs out.

'You won't feel a thing,' he said, unconvincingly I thought. I couldn't help being a bit nervous. Suppose the tongs got stuck, or broke off or something? In fact I'd been told they often fell out and I was lucky not to have had that happen.

The assisting nurse was looking at my worried face teasingly.

'Don't worry, Max. They'll be out in half an hour.'

'Half an hour?' but she was laughing.

'Well,' she relented. 'Maybe only twenty minutes.' She looked beyond my head to where Dr. Maynard was presumably standing, busy with the tongs, but at that moment I caught a glimpse of him out of the corner of my eye, dropping something metal on to a side cabinet.

I swivelled my eyes accusingly to the nurse. 'They're out, aren't they? The tongs are out!'

She nodded through her laughter, and I tried to take a swipe at her with my good arm. She ducked, and Dr. Maynard came over to confirm the tongs had slipped out without any difficulty.

'Now you must keep your head still for a while yet,' he instructed. 'You could undo two months' healing with one careless movement.'

He didn't have to warn me twice.

Back in the ward, the fellows yelled their congratulations

and I basked in an unreasonable sense of achievement. Tommy was a few days ahead of me, and I assured him I'd catch up before long.

''ear all your family's comin' at the weekend', Dave Pembury said cheerfully. 'Don't forget to introduce your ol' buddies now, will you?'

'Of course not,' I returned, excitement in my voice. I could hardly wait to see them now.

But the long-awaited hair wash had to come first. Hot, soapy water carried ceremoniously to the top of my bed. Polythene fitted carefully round my neck and down behind my head so the water would be channelled into a bucket. Then the gentle hands of a nurse washing all the filth away. Bliss! I felt like a king when it was done.

Saturday morning brought excited, running feet.

'Here we are, here we are,' sang Annie's voice from somewhere down beside my bed. Then, 'What a big bed. I can't climb up on it.'

'I can,' and Noddy was up on the other side in a second, a shy grin on her face and new ribbons in her glossy dark hair. It only took an appreciative comment from me about the ribbons to set her at ease, and she launched into telling me all her news just as she might have done on any evening at home when I'd come in from work. Annie joined in, perched where Susie had swung her near my elbow, her little hand in mine.

They seemed larger than life. I was sure they'd both grown in my absence. I listened to their chatter delightedly, relieved that my strange appearance didn't seem to frighten them. I was still practically bald where the tongs had been. Susie had obviously prepared them well, telling them in graphic detail what to expect. 'I even lay down on the floor and tried to look like you,' she confided with her deep, girlish laugh.

Only Ben didn't speak. He buried himself shyly in his mother's arms, and then clambered down to explore the ward. While we chatted on, he toddled over to Dave Pembury's bed and became fascinated with the bright red button he found at about his eye level. The next moment a muffled yell from Dave alerted us to Ben's discovery – he'd set the turning mechanism in motion on Dave's bed.

In the ensuing commotion, both Dave and Ben were rescued and the ward rang with laughter.

'I bet that wasn't quite the introduction you'd anticipated,' I called over to my neighbour when he'd got over the shock.

'No, that doesn't count,' Dave replied good-humouredly. 'I want a proper introduction now.'

It was rather a confused and red-faced little boy who finally said a tiny 'hello' to 'Mr. Pembury' from the safety of Sue's arms. Dave was delighted.

'And guess what, Daddy,' Annie broke in on her own conversation, obviously just remembering something very important. 'Gom has come to stay with us.'

'Has she?' I looked questioningly at Sue.

'She came last week,' Noddy added importantly. 'Mummy wanted it to be a surprise.'

It was certainly that. 'Gom', or Molly if she was being formal, had been nanny-cum-housekeeper for Justyn's sister for years. I didn't know she'd moved and was free to come to Pepperland.

'Another answer to prayer,' Susie said simply. 'She and Jennifer agreed that we could use her help, so she just decamped. Jen can manage on her own now the children are older.'

'She's very funny,' Annie added. 'Makes us laugh *all* the time.' She made her voice sing out for emphasis.

'That's wonderful,' I said to Susie as the children talked on about their new friend. She nodded, eyes sparkling.

'I'll have time to answer all your letters, and Gom can look after the children whenever I want to come and visit you. It's perfect. And she's a great companion too. The house doesn't seem so empty.' Sue's voice was sober just for a second.

'Oh I almost forgot,' bright again. 'There's something else. Your old school chaplain, Peter Hancock . . .'

Peter was assistant chaplain at the hospital now, and had

113

completely taken me by surprise the first time he visited me. I had no idea he was at Stoke. I remembered him for his disarming cheerfulness at school: he was always whistling some happy tune or smiling broadly. He didn't seem to have changed much. The same kindness was underneath. He'd become a real friend and support at the hospital, visiting me as often as his busy schedule allowed and keeping my spirits up.

'His wife Sue rang me up the other day,' Susie continued, 'and suggested I use their spare bedroom instead of the hostel when I come to visit you. You know they only live nearby.' She stopped for my reaction, but I was speechless.

'She wouldn't take no for an answer,' Sue finished.

I reached for her hand, and did my best to squeeze it.

# CHAPTER 8

Radio 1 was well into its stride and the ward loudly awake on the Wednesday morning Communion was first brought to my bed.

'Hello, Mr. Sinclair, I'm Canon Byard.'

I recognised the name of the hospital chaplain and looked up at a tall, clerical figure, standing rather incongruously beside my bed.

'Would you like Communion?' The figure smiled expectantly.

It was the lull between my bed bath and the linen change. I was scantily clad, and covered in baby powder after my wash, waiting for the lifting team to get round to me.

'Er yes,' I stammered, feeling more than a little foolish. 'Yes, I would.'

The Canon seemed quite unperturbed, and reached to draw the curtains round my bed. I'd requested to be included in the fortnightly administration of Communion, but this was one of the busiest times in the hospital routine. What sort of Communion . . .? But the Canon was bending his head in prayer, so I closed my eyes and tried to concentrate, hoping the orderlies wouldn't arrive suddenly to finish preparing me for the day.

As soon as the Canon's reverent voice began speaking the words I knew so well, I forgot about my strange situation and the music blaring across the ward. We shared a precious three minutes in our little curtained-off 'chapel', and they meant as much to me as any full-blown service in a church. It was the first time I'd had real privacy at Stoke to worship God, and He seemed all the closer because of it.

I didn't start reading the Bible again for myself until some weeks after Susie had gone home. Strangely enough, it wasn't the first book I reached for once I'd mastered the reading stand. I'd become so used to God's special upholding, the inner peace and continual sense of His presence, that I didn't think to get back seriously to the study of His Word.

It was only when Susie mentioned it one weekend that I realised my neglect.

'Are you reading the Bible, Max?' Her casual question surprised me. I'd asked visitors to the Hall the same thing many times, and it felt odd to be on the receiving end for once. I must have blushed as many of those others had blushed when I admitted that I hadn't really got back into it yet.

Chastened, I had my Bible fixed to the reading stand at the earliest opportunity, but it was a long time before I really got back into my old habit. The sense of God's nearness was still so strong it didn't seem important to maintain the discipline of daily Bible reading. I didn't realise what dangerous ground I was treading. God might provide special support during a crisis, but He wouldn't give it indefinitely. If I didn't build up my own resources

115

again, I'd be a prime candidate for Satan's deceptions. It took an incredible two years for me to learn my lesson and win the struggle to return properly to continual, regular study.

One time my Bible was propped above me, a new visitor approached.

'How d'you do, Max?' the white-coated young man smiled warmly as if he already knew me. 'I'm John Philips from the surgical ward just up the corridor.' He jerked his head in the appropriate direction, making his stethoscope jump on his chest.

'I hear you're from Hildenborough Hall,' he continued. Without anything else being said, I knew this was another Christian member of staff. It explained why John appeared to know me, and why I felt quickly at ease in his company too.

John nodded approvingly at my reading material.

'You know,' he said with his head on one side. 'Every time a Christian comes into a ward, things change.'

'Do they?' I replied rather blankly, not at all convinced that my presence in 2X would make a hap'orth of difference to the place.

'You'll see,' returned my knowing friend.

His words made me think. Did he mean I should be witnessing? I could understand that he might see the hospital as providing an ideal opportunity for sharing God's Word – I'd felt the same when I first went to Exeter. But the vicar there hadn't been of the same opinion.

'Max,' he'd said, shaking his head. 'You're here first to get better. Think of that and don't worry about witnessing.'

But there were people in need right beside me. Surely God meant me to tell them of Himself. It took me a while to realise the wisdom of the vicar's words. He meant me to see that I couldn't wear my 'Hildenborough Hall Evangelist' hat in hospital. The situations were so different, I couldn't just talk out of the blue about the love of God. The people around me weren't open and searching like I might find at Hildenborough. They were in pain, and probably highly sceptical about the existence of any God, let alone a loving one.

I'd decided then not to witness in the direct way I was used to. I would rely on God to show me how I could share my faith meaningfully.

Perhaps that's what John meant too, that God would 'use us' as Susie and I had prayed, simply because we were there and trusting Him.

And God did provide opportunities. Every time I was asked what I did, for instance, I was sharing my faith in some measure simply by speaking of the Hall and my work there.

Dave Alexander was the first to ask me in detail about Hildenborough.

'A Christian Conference Centre? You mean you get lots of folk together to read the Bible?'

'Well, yes and no.' I tried to think of the best way to describe the Hall. 'We do lots of other things too – we have a concert every Saturday night . . .'

'Really?' Dave interrupted, his voice eager. 'What kind of concerts are those Max?'

'All sorts. We have different artists each week.'

'Folk, jazz, pop?' Dave was obviously a music enthusiast.

'A bit of everything.' We had such a mixture, I couldn't pin it down to anything very specific. 'Our own band, Pace, does quite a few of the concerts, and that's guitar . . .'

'Great instrument, the guitar,' Dave said as I drew breath.

'. . . keyboards and vocals,' I finished.

'The guitar is what I really go for,' repeated Dave.

'Me too. I used to play myself.'

'*Did* you?' Dave sounded very impressed. 'Did you play much?'

'Quite a lot when I was younger, but less recently. One of the last times I played,' I was getting carried away with such a captive audience, 'was with Cliff Richard on a Saturday night at the Hall.'

No response for a moment.

117

'You're kiddin',' Dave said at last.

'It's true. I played while he sang . . .' I was interrupted by a roar of laughter from my neighbour. I'd lost any chance of telling him more about Bible study at the Hall.

'Hey fellas,' he called to anyone within earshot. 'Max here says he's played guitar for Cliff Richard.'

There were several chortles of disbelief from various quarters of the ward.

'I've never yet met a straight accountant,' Dave Pembury contributed scathingly.

He meant what he said, although I'd learnt by then not to take too many of his preconceived ideas personally. He found this side of me harder to take even than my Christianity – as did several others. The builders, dockers and second hand car dealers had never trusted the pin-striped City world.

There was something deeper breaking down those barriers in 2X however. A sort of 'fellowship of suffering' brought us close in a way we could never have been in any other situation. It was unique in my experience, and something I was already beginning to treasure.

'Ask him for proof,' someone yelled from the far end of the ward.

'Sue's got a photo of us,' I yelled back. 'I'll ask her to bring it so you can all see.'

'Could it be a fake?' Dave Alexander continued to tease.

'Just wait and see.'

The photograph was duly found, but even then the fellows weren't satisfied.

'Get away with you Sinclair, that's never you. And when did Cliff Richard look like that?' True enough, the picture *had* been taken from the back of the hall so the famous pair on the stage were rather small, but there was no doubting its authenticity.

I was finally granted my claim to fame.

'Oh well, so you're famous an' all,' Dave Pembury conceded reluctantly. 'Trust you!'

I laughed heartily. There was more acceptance of me in

118

that remark than in any that had gone before. I was delighted! Somehow, the Cliff Richard episode had pushed the dubious idea of me as an accountant into the background. It might even have shown Hildenborough Hall to be good fun too!

I was feeling much more at home in the ward by now. When Susie first left, everyone was so kind in stopping by my bed for a couple of minutes' chat on their way to visit someone else that I couldn't feel lonely for long. And getting to know the friends and relatives of the others helped me to feel more at ease with my fellow-patients too.

There were Mrs. Barrett and Tommy's girlfriend from Liverpool, both of whom spoke with such thick accents I could hardly understand what they said. I pretended I didn't know what they meant when they talked of 'jam butties' or 'scouse pies' – until Mrs. Barrett brought me some delicious samples to stop my joking. She was specially attentive to me somehow, perhaps because Tommy and I were at a similar stage of recovery. Perhaps too because of the bond that had been established between her and Sue when Sue gave her our jam-jar of rubbish-dump flowers. Sue had gone over on impulse to share our discovery because Tommy had been particularly ill that day, and the flowers had awakened a new hope in Mrs. Barrett too.

Dave Pembury's girlfriend was a regular visitor for a while, and often came across for a quick chat with me. Dave had introduced her proudly, but she looked a little embarrassed and never seemed quite at ease in the hospital. Gradually her visits became less frequent, until she stopped coming altogether. Dave never said anything, and I felt for him silently.

Now I joined in enthusiastically with the buzz of conversation that animated the ward. One of my first discoveries was that Dave Pembury loved fishing. He entertained me for hours with stories of rare catches, and insisted that I didn't know what I'd missed in not being a fisherman.

'You've got to try it, Max. Nothin' like it.'

I said I was sure he was right, but didn't manage to muster enough enthusiasm to please Dave.

'Take a lesson from Mrs. Carr,' he admonished. 'She knows a thing or two about fishin'. *She* agrees with me.'

Mrs. Carr, 'Grandpa's' widow, had spent fully half an hour talking fishing with Dave when she last visited me. He was bowled over.

'Fancy 'er botherin' to talk to me all that time,' he'd said several times after she'd gone. 'Real nice of 'er, that.'

That was one occasion Dave was impressed with something of Christianity. Words or ideas didn't get through to him, but someone's kind action did.

Feeling more alive and energetic than I'd done for weeks, I was impatient to move on. The next stage was sitting up, and I knew that would demand every ounce of my strength. I had to build up my resources. Not that I needed any excuse to eat everything that was put in front of me.

'Sinclair, do you like *everything* on the menu?' Dave said disparagingly one lunch time when I was congratulated on mopping my plate clean and he suffered a 'tut tut' for leaving something on the side.

'Everything.' My appetite had certainly returned with a vengeance after the deprivation of earlier weeks.

'Ward dustbin,' Dave announced drily. 'That's what we'll 'ave to call you. You and Ernie between you. You two eat more than the rest of us put together.'

'What was that?' the cracked, elderly voice of Ernie called from the other side of the ward. 'Is someone talking about me?'

Dave repeated the new name he'd found for us.

'Ah, that's a good one,' chuckled Ernie. 'That's a good one, isn't it, Max?'

'Fits just right,' I agreed.

Ernie was a sixty-four year-old builder's labourer who'd broken his neck after falling off a ladder. Before I even knew who he was, I knew his voice. Badly concussed when he first came to Stoke, he used to wake frequently in the night and call for the nurse to come and help him, convinced someone was trying to push him out of bed. It was almost grotesque, but once we'd got over our initial reaction we couldn't help seeing the funny side.

'Ernie, there's no one there,' was one tactic used to calm him.

'There is, there is,' Ernie would almost scream, and if the nurse persisted in trying to persuade him otherwise he would either burst into the most unprintable language or start crying like a child.

Chasing the 'bogey man' away was the only means of restoring peace to the ward.

'Shoo, be off with you,' or 'Will you stop bothering Ernie and go away,' or 'If I find you in this bed again . . .' became the most frequently used lines of attack. Eventually, perhaps after a particularly strong threat, the visitor disappeared completely and we enjoyed relatively undisturbed nights again.

Now Ernie responded good-humouredly to the teasing about his 'bogey man', in the same way as he laughed at being called one of the ward dustbins. He was endearingly cheerful.

There was another link between us beside our healthy appetites. Ernie was one of the two others who took Communion in the ward on Wednesday mornings. From the corner of my eye I could see the orange curtains being whipped round his bed after Canon Byard had left me. No mention of this had been made in our cross-ward conversation, when one evening Ernie surprised me.

'Good night, Max. God bless you.'

Coming as it did out of the blue, in a ward where anything reverent was rarely to be heard, Ernie's blessing touched me beyond words. Finding my voice, I called back the same greeting.

'Good night, Ernie. God bless you too.'

From then on, we exchanged these words every evening. Ernie called a cheerful good night to every one of his fellow-patients, but only to me did he add the blessing. It established a special bond between us.

121

As part of the preparation for propelling a wheelchair about, Rosemary introduced a new contraption to strengthen my hands and fingers. A piece of wood with elastic bands round it that strapped my fingers down. I had to try and pull the elastic away from the wood, using one finger at a time. No mean task.

Then I was given a piece of leather with holes punched in it to make myself a pouch. This would hang on the arm of my wheelchair and hold all the bits and pieces I wouldn't be able to keep in my trouser pocket in case of pressure sores. I was supposed to 'sew' it together by threading a leather thong through the holes. Rosemary showed me how, and then left me to it.

I tried first with my right hand, but couldn't even get hold of the thong, let alone push it through the leather. There was still no movement in my fingers, and my thumb wasn't strong enough to grip anything.

So it was a matter of reorientating myself to use my left hand. All the awkwardness of doing something the opposite way from what I was used to added to the problem of getting my fingers to move the way I wanted. When Rosemary came back, I hadn't advanced one bit.

'It would be better if I could see it,' I said in defence, although being able to see wouldn't have made my hands any more mobile. I'd tried holding the leather up above me, but had just dropped it whenever I transferred my attention to the thong.

'I know what we can do,' Rosemary cried suddenly. 'I'll find you some periscope glasses.'

I'd never heard of such things. I pictured long, unwieldy periscopes attached to ordinary spectacle frames, but Rosemary produced a pair of normal-looking glasses with just an additional 'hood' of carefully placed mirrors.

When I got them on, the ward was transformed! Instead of a view of the ceiling, I could see across to the row of beds opposite as if I were upright. There were all Tommy's get-well cards pinned up behind his bed, and a huge bunch of flowers in a vase next to him. Janie, his girlfriend, was putting the finishing touches to the arrangement.

'Hey Janie,' I called across in excitement. 'I can see you the right way up.'

She looked towards me in surprise. 'Did I used to be upside down then?' was her cheerful retort.

'I mean instead of at an angle. It's my new glasses.'

Just then, a nurse hurried down the ward, and I exclaimed with new delight at seeing someone walk 'normally' for the first time since the accident.

'Hey,' Rosemary tipped the magic glasses up off my nose and glared down at me in mock annoyance. 'You're supposed to be using these to make your pouch.' I'd forgotten all about that, and dutifully concentrated on trying again while Rosemary stood and watched.

By propping the folded leather up in my right hand, and grasping the thong in my left, I managed finally to make my first stitch.

Four days later, I'd completed my pouch. I'd alternated in that time between total frustration at my hands being so nearly useless, and excitement that something was being achieved, however slowly.

Once my fingers had strengthened, my hands were freed from their nightly 'boxing gloves'. Hearty congratulations from everyone, and a new surge of determination on my part to use my hands as much as possible. I tried first with my letters. If I gripped them tightly enough, I could yank the envelopes open with my teeth and then gradually manoeuvre what usually turned out to be a rather creased and crumpled page on to my reading stand. Being able to read the letters for myself gave me tremendous satisfaction. Until then, Maureen, our cheerful ward clerk, had always read them out to me, but I liked to be able to read leisurely, look back over things and consider what I might say in reply. It wasn't always easy, however. Sometimes, seeing the mess I made of the letters, I lost heart and let Maureen open them again and read them to me.

Writing my own letters was yet another matter. Sue was marvellous about answering all our early correspondence, but when she wasn't there, and I felt well enough to construct my own replies, I wanted to find a way of managing myself.

Once again, the kind Stoke Mandeville staff came to my rescue. Rosemary courageously volunteered to be my 'pen', to write as I dictated. We spent many an evening in collaboration, she scribbling frantically as I tried to answer as many letters as I could before my energy ran out. Our record was twenty letters in one go! To celebrate, we cut into two huge melons that had arrived that morning from our local grocer at home – the twentieth letter had been a 'thank you' to him. Everyone reckoned, between mouthfuls of juicy melon, that we ought to have marathon letter-writing sessions more often!

The dictating machine changed everything. It was Sue's idea, presented ceremoniously on one of her weekend visits.

'I felt sorry for Rosemary,' was her excuse.

It was marvellous, of course. It didn't take long to master the various buttons on the machine, and I basked in the new feeling of independence it gave me. Complete with the gift was the assurance of the secretarial skills of one of the staff at Hildenborough, so all I had to do was send off the finished tapes and my letters would be neatly typed and despatched. An unbeatable system.

It was just after one of my evening dictating sessions, during the final drug round of the day, that an incident occurred between me and Sister Clements which, rather surprisingly, brought us a lot closer in understanding.

That day, one of the junior nurses had been ill, so the others had been coping with extra work. I could tell Sister Clements was tired by the way she banged down my little plastic drug container so the pills rattled.

'Make sure you get those down you.' Her voice was more brusque than usual. She turned quickly to move on to the next patient, and that was when she knocked my pile of carefully-answered letters off the locker.

'Oh Christ!' she exploded, as if this was the last straw.

I couldn't contain myself.

'I'd rather you didn't say that near my bed.'

I think I was more surprised than she at my reaction! The words had come out spontaneously, but quite politely – in fact I sounded almost apologetic. As I heard my voice echoing in my mind, I was amazed that I'd spoken out at all.

'I – that name means a lot to me,' I added rather lamely.

'Why, yes – of course, Max,' Sister Clements found her tongue at last. 'I'm sorry.'

I was quite taken aback by this genuine apology. She could so easily have shrugged the whole thing off, or thought I was just being prudish. Instead, she seemed to appreciate why I was offended by her outburst.

As she walked away rather soberly, I hoped I hadn't offended *her* by what I said. But the next day, I was greeted on waking by a superb rendering of a classic Sunday School chorus:

'I am H.A.P.P.Y. . . .'

It was none other than Sister Clements, half-dancing up the ward to the accompaniment of her own voice.

'Sister Clements. Wherever did you learn that?'

She gave me a knowing wink.

'I was at Sunday School too, you know.'

For a split second, our eyes met, and then we both burst out laughing.

'Makes a change, eh?' said my warm-hearted Sister.

'Oh it does, it does indeed.'

From that moment on, Sister Clements showed a new respect for my faith, and I appreciated more fully her generosity and sensitive awareness of others. Chorus-singing became quite a feature of 2X – was this part of what John Philips envisaged when he told me a Christian changes things in a ward?

The next day, my wheelchair arrived. It had been ordered for me at the beginning of September. Now I was ready for it.

Every week, on Monday morning, Dr. Maynard came round the ward assessing each patient's progress. Those who were already up would disappear into his office for a few minutes, and emerge with great relief as if from an exam. Sometimes the news was good, sometimes not.

That Monday, four weeks after I was taken out of traction, I hung on the doctor's every word. As usual, we'd all tried to anticipate what he might say, whether he'd be encouraging or otherwise, whether he'd 'promote' any of us, change our drugs, or give the go ahead to a new stage – such as sitting up.

So often, there was no change at all, but this time, surely this time . . .

I felt the doctor's skilled touch along the back of my neck. 'Neck all right?' he queried in his abrupt, straightforward way.

'Fine.'

'Still keeping it straight? No movement?'

'Yes. No,' I responded dutifully, hoping he'd know which answer was meant for which question. Only a couple of days previously John Philips had crept up noiselessly and called a hearty 'Hello Max,' into my right ear. I'd stared resolutely ahead, resisting the temptation even to try and turn my head. I earned my friend's unbounded approval.

'Just testing,' he'd said mischievously.

'Well yes,' Dr. Maynard was moving away. 'I think we can have you X-rayed in a couple of days. You should be sitting up soon after that if all's well.'

My heart leapt. As soon as Dr. Maynard disappeared into his office, I let out a whoop of joy.

'Did you hear that, fellas? I'm going to sit up.'

'So am I,' Tommy called, equally excited. 'A week, perhaps.'

'Well good for you two,' was Dave Pembury's sarcastic comment.

'We'll stick together, Dave,' a slow, deliberative voice consoled from the other side of Dave's bed. 'We'll hold the fort.'

It was Boyd Parsons, or 'Postman' as we called him since he was a Post Office engineer. He objected to the nickname, which of course encouraged our teasing all the more. Boyd had broken his neck diving off a breakwater on Brighton beach into what he had thought was a deep pool. He'd made very little recovery.

'Yeah Postman,' Dave rejoined. 'We'll be the only ones left soon.' A pang of regret spoiled my own elation, but Dave soon thought of a way to even the score.

'Right Sinclair,' he yelled. 'Oim goin' to throw a grape at you.'

Entering into the spirit of this attack, I called back cheerfully, 'Okay – I could just do with eating one.'

A chorus of scepticism and delight greeted this remark. 'You'll never make it, Dave.' 'Open your mouth, Sinclair.' 'He'll want to go in for the Olympics next.'

'Got yer mouth open?' growled Dave.

'Yaahs' I returned emphatically, stretching my mouth wide.

'Ere it comes.' Dave's voice was triumphant, and to my astonishment a little dark shape hurtled straight into my mouth. I choked and spluttered to everyone's loud appreciation.

'How did he do it?' 'Can I have your autograph, Pembury?' 'Try another – Max needs building up.' All the tension of Dr. Maynard's visit was released. Grapes flew everywhere, and tears of helpless laughter poured down our cheeks.

The X-ray was scheduled for two days later.

'Steady Max,' Sister Clements tried to calm my excitement as she wheeled me to the X-ray department. 'This is only a check, you know. The bone may not be sufficiently healed yet.'

I hadn't even entertained such a possibility. Surely there would be no hold-ups now.

The machine clicked round me. Dr. Maynard looked sober.

'Another two weeks, Max. I'm sorry.'

I was stunned. It seemed a lifetime. Back in the ward, I couldn't trust myself to speak. It wasn't hard for the lads to guess what had happened, and no one attempted to console me. They all knew it was a disappointment no words could heal.

But I wasn't allowed to wallow in self-pity. Minutes later, Penny came up and whispered in my ear.

'Hey. How would you like to come to a party?'

I didn't feel very festive, but I'd never known a party to happen at Stoke Mandeville before.

'Is it your birthday?' I asked, wondering how I'd be able to get to a party anyway.

'No. One of the girls from the Christian fellowship is leaving next week, and we're just having a little get-together to say goodbye. I thought it might be a good chance for you to meet some of the others – as well as have some fun I hope.' Penny smiled.

'Well,' I began, touched by her thoughtfulness. 'I'd love to come – but the doctors won't like you moving me.'

'Don't worry. We'll arrange that.'

Halfway through the evening, Penny came in with two friends to whisk me away to the party. None of them were in uniform.

'Are we going out of the hospital?' I found myself asking.

''Fraid not. Only to the Physiotherapy Department. You'll have an early sight of where you'll spend much of your time eventually.' I was wheeled through a final set of swing doors into a large room full of apparatus: cycle beds, wooden bars, dangling arm slings.

'This is where everyone works while you have easy passive physiotherapy in bed,' Penny teased as she flipped the brake on my bed. 'But your turn will come.' I looked around the room. It was rather like an obstacle course. In the pit of my stomach, a childish apprehension stirred. What on earth might I be asked to do?

Around me were cheerful faces, already enjoying the evening's celebration. Plates of tempting-looking sand-wiches and sweets were laid out on a long table, and a tape recorder filled the room with the echoing tones of the Christian singer, Dave Pope.

'Welcome, Max. Good to meet you,' greeted me on all sides.

I felt accepted and at home at once, despite the fact that I was the only one there in a bed! We all chatted and ate, sang choruses and laughed together. It was a tonic.

'Thank you, Lord,' I prayed once I was back in the ward. I felt refreshed and at peace. Two weeks wasn't long to wait really, and gave me a chance to strengthen my muscles a bit more. God didn't make mistakes in His timing.

\*   \*   \*   \*   \*   \*

A different cloud appeared on the horizon around this time. My right leg and foot had developed a regular habit of jerking into spasm at the least provocation. They never failed to make their bid for independence when Ollie was trying to exercise them during our physio sessions. Even calm Ollie couldn't hide her exasperation at times.

'Here I am trying to loosen your muscles, and you're insisting on tensing them up again!'

But there was nothing I could do.

'How is it that just my right side is affected and not my left?' I asked her once.

'Because your brain can get the message through to your left side to stop the reflex action. The Brown Sequard Syndrome – remember? You've regained more movement down the left side of your body and have more control over it. But the right' – she looked crossly at my energetic foot – 'just goes its own way.'

Which might not have mattered except for the adverse effect on my foot. Every spasm in my calf muscle pulled my foot down almost parallel to the bed, and there it would stay even when the spasm was over. I couldn't pull it back up again. And while my foot pointed downwards, the tendon was relaxed and apparently in danger of adapting to the new position by growing shorter.

'You might end up with your foot permanently in that position,' wailed Ollie after a particularly long spasm.

'You mean locked like that?' I was suddenly worried.

'Well it can happen. You'd be surprised how difficult it is to stretch a tendon once it's contracted.'

The trouble was that every time Ollie or one of the other staff tried to ease my foot gently back up, the spasms would be set off again. A regular battle developed between my foot and the staff, and the staff were more often the losers.

What had begun as merely a nuisance was now a real cause for concern.

If I was ever to get as far as standing up, I would have to be able to place my foot flat on the ground.

'Let's try a plaster cast,' was Sister Clements' suggestion. It was rather disconcerting to realise that the staff knew little more than I did about how to solve this problem.

A cast was made to fit around the bottom of my foot and ankle, reaching half way up my calf. The top was open, so it could be slipped on and off easily. My foot was firmly held in its normal position.

'Well, that'll do the trick for the time being,' Ollie said. No one was very optimistic about how long this solution might last.

Tommy sat up before me.

'Go easy, go easy,' he shouted breathlessly as the top half of his bed was winched slowly up.

'Stop a minute. I'm getting dizzy.' I was lying flat, facing the ceiling, so I couldn't see what was going on. I just heard Tommy's sharply drawn breaths of anticipation, and his delighted exclamations once he got used to being able to view the world from a normal angle.

'I can see you over there, Nurse Ann. Are you trying to avoid giving me my coffee?'

I didn't know what Tommy looked like, but I imagined his face split with a wide grin and his eyes sparkling with excitement.

'Can you see us over here then, Tommy?' I said to the ceiling.

'Just the tip of your nose, Max old man. I'll have to wait till you sit up too.'

130

When it came to his getting into a wheelchair a couple of days later, there was even more excitement. After several dizzy protests, there was a sudden silence.

'He's fainted,' Boyd roared. 'Old Tommy's fainted.' This time I was tipped up on my side and saw poor Tommy's head flop to one side. Quick as a flash, the orderly holding the chair tipped it backwards so the blood could flow back to the top of his body. When Tommy came to, he was whipped smartly back to bed.

'I'll do better next time,' he defended himself hotly to his laughing fellow-patients. 'They say it always happens.'

Tommy wasn't the only one out of bed that day. A new visitor was wheeled round to my bedside. I didn't know who he was at first. Ruddy-faced, with little tufts of white hair and a toothless grin, his voice told me his identity.

'Ernie,' I exclaimed in delight. 'You're looking great.'

A huge grin crinkled his cheeks.

'Had to come and see you Max.'

Ernie's heavy, labourer's body sat inert in the wheelchair like a sack of potatoes. He'd recovered very little movement. His arms hung loosely, and his hands sat lifelessly in his lap.

'How does it feel,' I resumed, 'to be up at last?'

'Good, good.' There was a long pause before his next remark.

'You look fine too, Max.'

We didn't have to say much. There wasn't much to say. We were just glad to share each other's company.

Before many days had elapsed, both Tommy and Ernie had caught chest infections. That was one thing we were all prone to, and tried the most to guard against. Unable to cough normally and get rid of the phlegm, we were in considerable danger once the infection took hold. The two wheelchair pioneers were confined to their beds again, and I fought back a new wave of apprehension at the prospect of sitting up. I'd be just as likely to become ill, perhaps seriously.

Tommy picked up again after a week back in bed, but Ernie went steadily downhill. He was transferred to my old corner position so the nurses could come quickly to him if necessary. The curtains were kept drawn round him, so I couldn't even communicate with my old friend. Somehow, as I listened to his painfully-drawn breaths, I knew he was fighting for his life.

It was the evening before my second X-ray, and I was half way through my Daily Light portion, propping the battered little book on the pillow beside me to read. While my eyes were following the words, my mind was on that gurgling breath and Ernie's suffering.

Suddenly it struck me that Ernie might like to hear some verses of Scripture. Would he be able to hear me though, through the curtain and above the few radios that were still playing? As I realised I'd have to shout quite loud, I became embarrassed at the thought of the others hearing me too. Perhaps it would be better just to keep quiet. Ernie probably ought not to be disturbed anyway.

But my conviction to share the Daily Light verses with him persisted. Finally I took the plunge.

'Ernie, can you hear me?'

I had to assume that the indecipherable grunt that interrupted Ernie's torturous breathing meant yes. At least he was conscious.

'I've been reading my Daily Light for this evening. Would you like to hear some of the Scripture verses?'

Another grunt came from behind the curtain.

'Okay, here we go.' I'd read him two of the verses, grouped under the heading 'Affliction', when Dave Pembury called over to me.

'I don't think 'e can 'ear a thing, Max. Too much noise.'

I was flustered at this interruption. My voice was obviously audible to everyone, and I couldn't know if Ernie was understanding me or not. But I persisted to the last verse, from Deuteronomy 33 verse 27, 'The eternal God is thy refuge, and underneath are the everlasting arms.'

'There's something to think about as you go to sleep, Ernie,' I shouted after a pause. 'Good night and God bless you.'

Words were still too much for Ernie to manage, but I imagined what he was trying to say was his usual good night. I was glad I'd read to him, embarrassment or not.

Our nightly ration of pills was given out, and the 11.00 p.m. turn brought me back to face the ceiling. The lights had been out barely ten minutes when Ernie's struggling breath suddenly ceased. The silence was loud in the darkness. Was someone going to come and pump his chest, or . . . I stared frozenly at the ceiling, not wanting to believe that Ernie might have lost his battle to live.

Footsteps and the soft tinkle of the curtain rings. A light just over Ernie's bed. I heard them washing his body.

The corner bed was empty the next morning. The metal frame and rubber mattress were ugly, impersonal. All that was left on the locker was a vase of roses, strikingly warm and colourful. My eyes were drawn to them, and a sense of the enduring beauty of God's handiwork came to me through the sadness of death.

The whole ward was subdued. It was two years since anyone had died in 2X.

'How'd it happen, Max?' was the question I was posed several times. There was nothing I could say except that I'd read to Ernie at the crucial last moment. I think they appreciated the significance of that and were moved by it as much as by the death itself. What had prompted me to read to him just then? I was awed by the thought that perhaps God was comforting him, preparing him somehow for eternity.

'Are you ready for your X-ray, Max?' Sister Clements roused me from my thoughts. She spoke kindly, knowing I was already regretting that I wouldn't be able to visit Ernie in my wheelchair.

I looked back at the roses as we moved out of the ward. They were very beautiful.

# CHAPTER 9

'Give me a shout if you find you can't move again.'

Hemmed in by the X-ray machine, my eyes widened in panic at the doctor's casual words. He was skilfully positioning my head, turning it one way and another, while I waited for the horrifying shock of paralysis once more.

'Fine, Mr. Sinclair,' reassured the doctor finally. 'No nerves trapped there. Your neck has healed very nicely.'

I had to be moved to a different bed to sit up. My old one didn't have the necessary hinge in the middle. I was wheeled several places up the ward, to the accompaniment of 'unfair promotion' and 'preferential treatment' from my fellow-patients.

''ave you been bribin' them again, Sinclair?' yelled Dave Pembury.

'I am seriously going to get myself a spade,' said Tommy. He'd been in the same place for two months and decided the only way to get out of 2X was to dig a tunnel!

Slowly lifted from my lying-down position, I felt like a child with a new toy as I viewed the world from a normal angle at last. I was only at about twenty-five degrees, but it seemed I could see for miles.

'Boyd, is that really you?' He was still on his back and couldn't see me, but he grinned at my shout.

'Oi expect it's me.' It was amazing to fit the voice I'd known for so many weeks to the tanned face and mop of black, curly hair.

'And Tommy!' A slim-faced, pale young man was waving to me from the other side of the ward.

'Good to see you, Max old chum.'

I thought of the man in the Bible who'd had his eyes opened by Jesus, able to see people for the first time when before he'd only known voices.

It was thrilling.

The sun shone through the window opposite, and I could see grass and trees outside. I even watched a car go past and felt really excited by that one small thing. Soon I might be able to go out myself. Susie's cousin, John Church, had promised me a trip in his new BMW.

But even at this stage, I couldn't assume anything. On the fifth day, just before I was due to be lifted into my wheelchair, the doctors found a suspicion of a pressure sore. I was told I'd have to stay lying down for a while.

Oh no, Lord. Surely I'm not going to have to wait even longer. Turned painfully from one side to the other, I reminded myself that setbacks could happen any time. I was no more exempt from them than anyone else. I was still dependent on God for every forward step.

Lord, help me accept your will, and give me patience.

Only one day was lost. At the end of it, the staff satisfied themselves that no pressure sore was developing, and I had butterflies all night in anticipation of the wheelchair.

Susie was there to see it all. I didn't faint, or fall out, but I was glad to get back into bed after a quarter of an hour. It was incredibly tiring just to hold myself upright.

Dear Susie had brought strawberries – in the middle of winter! – to celebrate.

The next day I was allowed half an hour in the chair, and then a whole hour. My neck was supported by a close-fitting plastic collar which Rosemary had made for me.

'It'll help just till your neck muscles get stronger,' she'd told me. 'You won't need it for long.'

I began to try my hand at propelling myself about, precariously balanced, with as straight a back as I could manage. I'd got as far as Boyd's bed one afternoon when Laurie, one of the orderlies, rushed over and announced he was going to take me for an excursion. He spun my wheelchair round and headed for the doors at what seemed a fantastic pace. I don't suppose it was very fast really, but I wasn't used to any kind of movement.

'This is the archery room,' said my guide as we pushed

our way through some swing doors. We slowed to a halt, and I relaxed my efforts to hold on to the chair.

'You can see by the holes in the ceiling that not everyone reaches the standard of a Robin Hood.' Laurie pointed upwards. Tentatively, I bent my head back and saw what he meant. There were several marks where arrows had gone off course.

On we went to the hydrotherapy swimming pool, a huge oblong of water in a warm, steamy room. Everything seemed to reflect the blue water.

'You'll be in here soon, I expect,' Laurie said. 'You see that contraption over there? The plastic chair? You'll sit in that to be lowered into the water.' We went round for an inspection.

'But I won't be able to swim,' I lamented.

'The physios will help you. You'll be surprised what you can do with the water buoying you up.'

Excitement mounted inside me. I'd always loved swimming. Born on the coast, Bernard and I swum almost before we'd walked. We used to chase the incoming waves, see who could stay underwater the longest, have races.

I was enjoying the tour now. So much more to the hospital than I'd realised. A shop, a canteen, a lounge where patients could bring their guests for a quiet change of scene. There was even a little kitchen attached with a kettle for brewing up tea or coffee.

'Jimmy Savile helped provide this,' informed Laurie. 'We call it the Jimmy Savile lounge.'

I'd often seen Jimmy around the hospital. He usually wore a track suit, and managed to be very unassuming despite his celebrity status. We had an amusing encounter one evening when I was phoning Susie, still confined to my bed at that time. I'd just dialled the number when Jim popped up and asked to be put on the line. I handed him the receiver, and he launched into a characteristic opening gambit.

'Hello. What's your name. I fancy you.'

Sue must have told him her name.

'Why aren't you down here with your old man then?'

I imagined Sue said something about the children, but she wasn't going to get away with that excuse.

'Oh don't worry about them,' was Jim's reply. 'Just pop them in the fridge – they'll keep till you get back.'

On the way back to the ward, Laurie stopped my wheelchair near a window.

'Look at this,' he said with an air of having saved the best till last. He pointed out to a little garden, with neatly cut grass and a winding concrete path. Pink and yellow roses were planted along the edge of the path, and the whole picture moved me with its natural, fresh beauty.

'I haven't seen anything so lovely since I've been here.'

'I knew you'd like it,' Laurie replied simply. There was suddenly a deeper bond of friendship between us. I was amazed and touched by his perceptiveness, by how well he'd got to know me. I didn't feel so daunted by what lay ahead either after our little excursion. It seemed there was plenty to enjoy, whatever other demands might be made.

But the work began at once. My first day in the Physiotherapy Department confirmed my earlier apprehension. A hive of grim-faced activity, it was relieved by the good humour and encouragement of my new physiotherapist, Ebba.

'Max, don't look so worried,' she laughed when we arrived. It was a high-pitched, ringing laugh that transformed her otherwise serious face and dispelled the air of authority I'd found rather awesome at first. I was soon to discover how often this laughter bubbled to the surface, and how infectious it was.

'Now we are just first going on this little bench to sit.' There was an unusual inflexion to her voice, and a curious order to the words she spoke – enough to give away her Swedish nationality.

'Are you ready?'

She enlisted the help of one of the other physios and together they lifted me out of my wheelchair on to the bench. Ebba sat down quickly next to me 'in case you fall over'. I felt rather put out that she didn't think I could hold myself up on a bench, until she moved over a little and I nearly lost my balance. Even with her beside me it was all I could do to stop myself toppling over. No chance to think about posture. I was exhausted after five minutes.

'That's good for a start,' Ebba said when I was back in my wheelchair. But I only felt small and humiliated that I couldn't even manage something simple.

Occupational therapy was less gruelling. Rosemary sat me in front of a desk with a pencil and paper, and instructed me to 'write anything you like'. After an hour or so, I'd managed 'Help' in large, spidery left-handed script.

In our next session, I managed to compose a letter to Susie. My writing was huge, like a child's first attempt, and only a few words filled a whole sheet of paper. Halfway through, I'd despaired of finishing it, so badly was my hand aching. I'd slumped back in my wheelchair and looked up from the page, out of the window. Bright sunlight was spilling over the sill, and painting gold the edges of cloud in the sky. A surge of new encouragement made me take up the pen again. There was a power far greater than my own animating the world, a power I could draw on.

I learnt one-handed typing next, with a wooden 'finger' strapped to my hand to bonk the keys. I'd always been a great one for writing things down. I used to start each day at the Hall with a notepad and list everything I had to do in order of importance. There were three categories: things that had to be done at all costs, those I hoped to do and those that could wait until tomorrow. More often than not the day finished with only a few items in the first category completed.

Anything I had to remember, I would write down. If something struck me as interesting or funny, I would find a scrap of paper and note it. Any decision of consequence that had to be made would find me weighing up the pros and cons in written columns. It was hard to get used to the loss of my pen and paper habit.

What I missed most of all was being able to supplement my reading with notes. My pen usually scattered itself freely over the page of a book. Good bits were underlined. Funny bits had exclamation marks next to them in the margin. Scribbled comments appeared everywhere: 'absolutely right', 'I don't follow this' or 'complete rubbish'. All this helped me to latch on to the writer's train of thought, and without it I found serious works infuriatingly just out of my grasp.

Even my own thoughts seemed less clear when I couldn't commit them to paper as I was used to doing. So it was tremendous to be able to use a typewriter – but still so slow. It was quite an effort to hit the right key hard enough once I'd located it, so I didn't achieve much during my allocated hour and a half of Occupational Therapy.

Then the electric typewriter arrived. What a difference! It was a gift from some of the many folk continuing to pray for us, and transformed my painful writing process. A touch of the keys was enough to make the type appear on the page. A whole stream of correspondence was begun to my friends who'd had to put up with second-hand letters while I relied on Rosemary or the dictating machine. I was in my element.

I didn't have quite the same success with the wood-turning. My clumsy, stiff-handed efforts reminded me of my first encounter with carpentry at school. In woodwork classes, I'd painstakingly tried to master the technique of sawing a piece of timber off square or planing an edge to an exact measurement. The correct process always seemed an inordinately long one, and I would usually attempt some short cut – much to the chagrin of my teacher. I rarely got anywhere any faster, and spent several hours undoing the results of my misdemeanours.

I can only recollect turning out three finished products at this early stage. One was an oak book stand which miraculously is still intact, while the other two were somewhat faulty in design and eventually died quiet deaths. The coffee table sat proudly in our sitting room at home until the evident weakness in its legs became too much of a liability. It had a tendency to fall to the floor if someone as much as sneezed from the other side of the room. One day it just wasn't there any more. I didn't really question it, since a number of our much-loved family pets had 'gone away on holiday' and 'liked it so much they stayed'. The table had obviously followed suit.

The last product of my imaginative talent, a garden bird table, reached the heights of a prize exhibit on Open Day. But it had a hidden weakness, which one knowing school-fellow had already pointed out when I was applying the last touches of paint.

'Paint is no good on bird tables,' he said. 'It will soon peel off, and you'll have to paint the whole thing again.'

I looked scornful.

'Paint is a very good wood preservative,' I repeated what I'd learnt.

The other was heedless of my words. 'If you don't repaint it when necessary,' he warned loftily, 'the wood will rot and collapse.'

I decided to ignore this young know-all, obviously out to annoy me.

For some months, the brightly-painted table was enjoyed by the bird population of our garden. When the paint started peeling off I was too busy with other things to re-do it, and the wood soon rotted from the damp. What was left of the sound timber was quite useful as firelighting material.

*   *   *   *   *   *

After several sessions, the first hurdles in physiotherapy were passed too. I learnt to balance on the bench, to flex my arm muscles and pull down weighted slings fitted round my wrists. I went in the hydrotherapy pool almost every day, and was amazed at how much smoother and better my movements were under water.

But when it came to standing up, we met a real obstacle – my foot! It pointed downwards so obstinately I couldn't get it flat to bear my weight.

Ebba took charge of the situation.

140

'We'll hoist you up from your chair, while someone holds your foot flat on the ground.'

It was worth a try, and a team of helpers rallied round. Soon my screams of agony mingled with their screams of laughter, and we ended up in a breathless heap on the floor, resigned to failure.

'Something will have to be done,' Ebba concluded ominously. The plaster cast had outlived its usefulness, cracking repeatedly under the strain of my continuing spasms.

'I think we'll have to cut that tendon.'

An operation? My heart sank.

'It's the only solution,' the specialist confirmed after examining my foot. 'Better that than not being able to stand,' he added kindly. 'Don't you agree?'

I could only cling to their assurances that the operation wasn't a difficult or serious one, that I really would be better off to have it. But my reviving optimism once again suffered a blow.

'You won't get further than three,' Ebba teased after the anaesthetic had been injected. I screwed up my eyes against the bright lights of the operating theatre and looked protestingly at my physiotherapist. I'd insisted before that I would still be awake when the operation began, half-disbelieving that the anaesthetic would work so quickly and half-frightened that it wouldn't have the desired effect on me. Resolutely, I started counting out loud.

'One, two, three . . .'

A dull, throbbing pain and a huge bandage was all that proved to me anything had been done at all. I was back in my bed in 2X, semi-conscious still and wondering how long this would keep me prostrate. I could hardly believe it when tall, gangly Ebba appeared at my bedside and announced I'd be standing before the day was out.

'It's important you don't allow your foot to get stiff,' she explained. Then, 'Don't worry. I'll help you.'

Clinging tightly to her, and biting back my tears of pain,

I stood some two or three hours later. Both my feet were flat on the ground.

I loved the new independence my wheelchair gave me. It was a delight to choose to visit someone, and stay chatting as long as I wanted to.

'Twenty minutes, Max,' I would be reminded regularly by one of the nurses, the cue for me to raise myself from the chair just a little way for as near a minute as I could manage. This was to reduce the chance of pressure sores forming at the base of my spine. It was a necessary, but difficult, task. I developed a way of leaning on one of the arms of the wheelchair, thereby transferring my weight as required without sapping all my energy.

'You're getting pretty strong there, Max,' old Lesley Harding would say every time I hoisted myself up in the chair while visiting him. 'How about lighting me a cigar?'

Lesley had established a reputation in the ward for his love of cigars. Anyone who would, or could, light one up for him was his friend for life. He couldn't move his hands at all, so was dependent on someone helping him if he wanted to smoke.

The first time I agreed to the task, it proved a near-calamity. I had to hunt through the bottom of his locker for the matches, which brought me dangerously close to toppling out of my wheelchair, and then I fumbled for ages trying to get a match out of the box and puzzling how to strike it. At last, with the box wedged against the arm of my wheelchair, the match flared.

Les puffed majestically. 'Aren't we clever,' he breathed, contented. But the match still burned, already close to my fingers. I couldn't shake it out like I used to, and at the last second I remembered to blow. It dropped on to the sheet. I stared at it in relief, recognising with a jolt of apprehension the potential danger in my handicap.

I felt even closer to the lads now I could see them, talk to them, and share more fully in the life of the ward. I ate at the table, sitting up normally with the others. It was incredible how satisfying, how restoring it was to drink

142

straight from a cup rather than through a straw. And even if I couldn't always manage to spear a piece of meat, or keep peas on my fork, it didn't matter because everyone else was having similar difficulties. Meal times became occasions of uproarious laughter.

But there was another side to being in a wheelchair which offset the advantages I was enjoying. Wheelchairs were nothing out of the ordinary in a hospital, but it seemed as far as the remote outside world was concerned I now qualified as a disabled person. My social worker, a quiet individual with whom I was never quite relaxed because it was rather odd to have to be 'social-worked', brought several forms for me to fill in: an application for a 'mobility allowance', something else called an 'attendance allowance' and finally – the last nail in the coffin – the form to put me on the Register of Handicapped Persons. My number was: 07/05/20249.

From feeling I'd made huge progress getting to a wheelchair at all, I found myself labelled again, stuck. I was relegated to a 'wheelchair status'. It was like finding yourself in a cul-de-sac when you thought the road led somewhere. Since my writing was still barely legible at that time, Sue had to fill in the forms for me anyway. The point came home to me even more strongly. I was dependent, and perhaps would always be so.

For the first time, I began to feel apprehensive about facing the world outside the hospital. There was a security in the company of my fellow-patients, based on mutual understanding and acceptance. But outside I would be an oddity, a handicapped person. I didn't like to think about it.

The promised trip in the new BMW was arranged one Saturday soon after I'd graduated to my wheelchair. It was a bright, crisp morning, and Sue staggered into the ward with a huge picnic basket for our country celebration.

'It'll probably be too cold to sit outside,' she apologised. 'But I thought a picnic would be fun anyway.' Picnics were a tradition in our family. At the slightest excuse, we'd make one up and pile into the car for an excursion. At the prospect of one today, I felt as excited as a schoolboy going on his first class outing.

John drew up outside the French windows. Tall, lanky and smiling, he helped me out of my wheelchair into the car. The air was cold but exhilarating. I took huge, delighted breaths.

'All right, Max?' John secured the seat belt, and slammed the passenger door. The smell and feel of the car jogged awake an old and dormant memory. For a moment I saw myself driving again, then lying in Susie's arms waiting for the ambulance. The picture quickly slipped back into the past as the others climbed into their seats and John started the engine.

'She's a really smooth runner,' he said proudly.

I was distracted from replying by my first glimpse of Stoke Mandeville from the outside. I stared at the straggle of barracks through the windscreen, and wondered how anyone could have made the place out to be a mansion!

'Okay, here we go.' John eased the car down the long drive, and I leant instinctively back in my seat. As we turned into the road, and then up a lane into the depths of the country, I felt as if I was on some fairground switchback. Everything rushed by in a blur, and the car seemed to sway in all directions. The others were chatting animatedly, but I didn't have any breath to join in the conversation.

'How do you like her, Max?' I heard John say.

'Lovely,' I managed. 'But, aren't you going a little fast?'

He was driving very slowly in fact, but it didn't seem that way to me.

'I'm just glad he's not going at his usual speed,' contributed his wife from the back.

'Don't worry. Max,' John reassured. 'I'm taking it easy. How about some music?' He flipped a switch on the dashboard and loud chords of Beethoven boomed out of a hidden speaker. Sue made some polite, appreciative comment, rescuing me from the effort of having to shout above the music as well as concentrate on staying upright in my seat.

As I got used to the speed of the car, I began to make out shapes of trees and other landmarks outside. Every time something loomed too close, or a car flashed by on the other side of the road, I flinched and caught my breath in fright.

'How far shall we go?' I heard John say.

'Let's stop soon, shall we?' Sue's welcome voice replied. She knew how I was feeling.

Another turn, and I was suddenly being jolted about all over the place.

'Bit bumpy, I'm afraid,' apologised John, 'but there's a lovely view on the other side of this wood.' I was jerked from side to side like a puppet. The seat belt was all that prevented me from toppling over completely.

'Here we are – right on the edge of the Chilterns.' We drew to a halt. 'And don't you agree about the view?' John turned to me.

'Oh yes, perfect,' I heard myself say. And with relief, 'You've got a fine car.'

'I thought everything coming the other way was going to crash into us,' I said later to Susie.

Sue's mouth twitched, and then she giggled. Catching her eye, I grinned too, and she burst into little explosions of laughter.

'It was really – very funny,' she said breathlessly. 'You sitting there trying to look as if you were enjoying yourself when really you were terrified.'

'You'd have been frightened too if you hadn't been in anything faster than a wheelchair for three months,' I defended.

It took a long time for me to feel safe in a car again. I didn't trust anyone at the wheel, whoever it was. We always seemed to be going too fast, or without enough care. But there was no haunting memory of the orange Capri looming in front of us, or the terrible moment of desperate effort to turn the Baracuda out of its path. I began to treasure the thought of driving again myself. Then, at least, I could handle the car as I wanted to instead of feeling resentful towards my chauffeurs.

November was nearly over when I plucked up courage to ask Dr. Maynard whether I might go home for a weekend. I felt well enough, and longed to bridge the gap that had widened over the months between Stoke and Pepperland. Home seemed so remote now, a different world.

'I'll have forgotten what it looks like if I don't go back soon,' I said to the doctor.

He granted permission unhesitatingly, and then looked at me quizzically over his glasses.

'Your faith has been a real support to you, hasn't it?' he said out of the blue.

I was too surprised to reply.

'You're one of the lucky ones,' the doctor added, almost to himself, bending his head back to the papers on his desk.

That was the only allusion Dr. Maynard made to my faith, but I understood him to mean I was lucky to have reason to hope. He recognised the importance of psychological as well as physical recovery.

'If someone doesn't want to recover,' I'd heard him say before, 'he won't. Just as, if someone thinks he won't be able to cope with a handicap, he won't be able to.'

I too had heard accounts of those who couldn't adapt to the 'outside world' – and one who had completely recovered physically – and had chosen to end their lives. They'd lost hope.

I was sobered by Dr. Maynard's words, and silently grateful again to the God who'd brought me safely this far.

Sue arrived on the Thursday evening, ready to take me home on Friday. I plied her with questions about the children, the neighbours, the Hall, needing to get my bearings again after so long away.

'Nothing's changed really,' she said. 'You'll see when you get back.'

The next day, I was tense in the passenger seat, instinctively closing my eyes against every oncoming car. Sue drove slowly and carefully, understanding my nervousness, but every so often my fright brimmed over into irritation.

'You're too near the middle of the road. Can't you pull

over?' or, when Sue accelerated to overtake, 'No, not now. There's a car coming. Stay back.'

An awkward silence followed such remarks. They were the first hint of how my fears and apprehensions were going to interfere with our relationship.

We hadn't been on our own together since the accident. We talked hard, but somehow I found it hard to communicate to Sue what the last couple of months at Stoke had really been like. She wanted very much to understand, to be close to me in the experience, but my attempts to explain seemed curiously inadequate. It didn't sound right to say I'd enjoyed the activity of recent weeks, or to speak of my apprehension about facing the 'real' world again. Equally, I couldn't appreciate all her homely activities quite like I used to.

It would take time, I told myself, to retrace together all the ground that had been covered in our separate worlds. For the moment, it was just going to be good to be home again.

As we completed the last few miles, I realised how tired and stiff I felt. Perhaps I would be able to rest this afternoon, stretched out on our comfortable sofa in the sitting room.

Round the corner at the top of the hill, and then left through our gateway. The house peeped through the leafless trees and then stood before me in all its glory. I wanted to sit gazing at it for a long time, soaking in the fact that I was home.

Almost before the car had stopped, the children were running out to welcome us. They hugged and kissed me, trying to tell me all their news in one go, then stood back rather bemused while Sue got my wheelchair out of the back of the car and laboriously helped me into it. Sunny dog barked madly all the time, as if uncertain whether this was friend or foe.

With a good deal of puffing over the back door step, I was propelled into the kitchen. Warm, with a smell of baking and days long ago, it was festooned with a childish 'Welcome home Daddy' in bright colours on sheets of paper stuck

147

together with Sellotape. Noddy and Anna seemed quite unperturbed to see me in a wheelchair, but Ben kept his distance, looking suspiciously at me as if wondering whether to believe I was really his daddy.

Sue was still busily unpacking the car when I noticed the trickle of blood on my hand. I stared at it in growing horror. When could I have scratched myself? Scrambling out of the car perhaps. But I hadn't felt a thing.

I was still looking, aghast, at my hand when Sue came in with armfuls of luggage.

'What's the matter?' She peered at my hand. 'Oh, it's just a scratch. I'll get a tissue to wipe it clean.'

In a moment, the blood was washed away, revealing a harmless, tiny scratch. I was shaken by the thought that something much more serious could have happened, and I might not have known. I was helpless to protect myself. The magnitude of that problem hit me for the first time.

'Don't look so worried,' Sue said. 'It's really not serious,' It wasn't until later that I found words to explain what was really the matter.

'We'll just have to be careful,' Sue tried to reassure me. How could she know the gnawing fear within me, the humiliation of being so vulnerable?

I didn't get my sleep on the sofa that afternoon. Noddy wanted me to see her drawings, Annie wanted to have rides in the wheelchair, perched on my lap, and Ben continued to disconcert me by his long, silent looks. By the end of the day, my body was aching so much I longed to go to bed. I could hardly hold my fork at tea time, and was acutely conscious of the children's curious glances at my efforts. Sue tried her hardest to be sensitive to how I was feeling, but I only felt miserable that I wasn't managing very well.

It was a relief to sit quietly by the blazing fire while Sue put the children to bed. I found myself thinking of the future with dull pessimism. How would I bath little Ben now? I couldn't even bath myself. And all the household chores – Sue would have to cope on her own. I might almost be still in hospital, so little could I contribute.

Tiredness and a sudden wash of self-pity prevented me from accepting the support and consolation Sue tried to offer me. We sat quietly together by the fire, talking a little, but keeping our different hurts and confusion buried underneath.

I was almost glad to be heading back to Stoke on Sunday. There, I could sleep when I needed to, be sociable when I wanted to, and not have to cope with any demands other than the goals I set myself. There were no sharp corners on which to cut myself, and no embarrassments about being in a wheelchair.

But I longed to be with my family, to come home permanently.

## CHAPTER 10

'Why don't we have a 'Pace' concert?'

It was Penny who spoke. The rest of the Christian Fellowship leaned forward eagerly.

'That's a great idea.'

'Everyone would love it.'

We'd been discussing how we could best share our faith with those around us. The subject had come up a number of times during our Bible studies, which I'd attended regularly since my graduation to the wheelchair. On several occasions, I'd been surprised to find the others looking to me for the exposition of a certain passage. Perhaps the title of Conference Director at Hildenborough Hall had given them the idea that I knew a lot about the Bible, but I couldn't help being glad to contribute something to Stoke at last. A little more of my former identity was creeping back.

'Will they be able to come, Max?'

'Well . . .' I tried to remember what their schedule was as Justyn had outlined it to me. They were always busy, but perhaps if we asked them to come mid-week . . . My thoughts whirled round the idea of Pace at Stoke Mandeville. The men would never have seen anything like it.

'I don't see why they shouldn't come if they're free,' I ventured. There was a babble of response.

'We could use the Physiotherapy Department.'

'I'll do some posters.'

'Max, you'll have to sing with them as you used to.'

Once the idea had taken hold, no one could let it drop. The more I thought about having the team, the more I became excited. There wasn't much going on in the evenings normally. I'd heard there was a bowls club somewhere with a bar, although I'd never been able to work out how men at various stages of paralysis could manage to play bowls. Apart from this, and a film shown every Thursday night, there were no evening activities. I knew even a Christian band would be welcomed with open arms.

'Right then, I'll get in touch with Justyn and see what can be arranged.'

It was settled in no time. Pace were not only free to come, but were eager to play at Stoke. Justyn enthused on the phone.

'Glad to hear you're back on form, Max old man. Marvellous idea. Keep 'em coming.'

Thursday, November 24th was set for the great occasion. Penny put posters up everywhere, calling Pace a 'Folk/Rock group' and the Hall a 'Christian Youth Centre'. She also stuck my name in brackets at the bottom, so complete strangers wandered in and out of 2X looking for me to ask what all this was about. I knew the word was getting around, and that people were enthusiastic to come along and investigate this curious team from somewhere called Hildenborough Hall. Perhaps we'd have a packed house.

But even I wasn't prepared for the turn out that evening. The concert was billed for eight o'clock, but people started

150

gathering well over an hour beforehand. Wheelchairs, patients unsteadily on foot, doctors, nurses – even a few beds squeezed into the corners. I began to get worried that the band wouldn't have enough room.

There was a huge mirror running along the back wall, and Pace's glittering instruments and equipment were reflected impressively. It seemed that the room was even fuller than it really was with everyone's reflections staring back at them.

I sat near the front, on the edge of my wheelchair with excitement. Such an opportunity for folk to hear about Jesus. It was thrilling too to see the young people I'd interviewed so many months before actually together as 'Pace'. I'd never seen them in action.

Susie stood beside me. She'd come up with Justyn and the team, ready to take me home the next day for another weekend.

The music couldn't have been better, and Justyn's five minute message at the end was just right – gave everyone something to think about. I don't know what the reaction was to the song Justyn made me come up and join in with, but it certainly provided considerable amusement. I would doubtless be teased by the lads after this.

The end of an evening's lively entertainment so often seems an anti-climax. The lights go up, and normal, everyday sounds take the place of the music, the play or whatever. But not this evening. I was sitting innocently in my chair, chatting to Susie and the folks from the Hall, when something bounded up and enveloped me in a bear hug.

'Max, Max,' said the something, identifying itself eventually as the large frame of my pool physio, Erica. Her face was flushed, with traces of tears still around her eyes. But she was smiling fit to launch the Queen Elizabeth.

'Max, I've come back to the Lord.'

Surprise must have been written all over our faces, for Erica went on quickly. 'I . . . I was quite a committed Christian before, you see. But the last year or so, it hadn't meant much. Until now.' She turned to J. 'I knew what you were talking about just then. And . . . well, I just wanted to thank you.' She couldn't go on for the emotion in her voice.

We sat together for ages, just sharing and talking, praising God.

It wasn't until later we learnt what special concern God had shown Erica that evening. Some months afterwards, she had to face the deaths of both her parents, and with her renewed faith she was able to cope in a way she'd never have done before. In a letter to us from Australia, she reiterated her thankfulness at having found again the source of her hope.

It was a long time before the memory of the concert faded. Everyone seemed to have enjoyed it, and some were quite challenged. The odd hesitant question about how long I'd been at Hildenborough, or whether I'd enjoyed being in Pace, opened the way to the deeper, hidden questions about God and what He could do for people who faced the future in a wheelchair.

'Why doesn't your God get us all out of here then, Max?'

Dave Pembury had often thrown this at me, and I'd never managed to answer it to his satisfaction – perhaps because he wasn't really open to hearing what I had to say. But this time, there was a heartfelt plea behind the words. Dave was stricken with a serious kidney infection, not sure whether he'd come out of it alive.

'Why's God doing this to me, Max? You're always saying He cares. Why's He doing this to me?'

I was so conscious of Dave's helpless sobs, his pain-racked, sweating body, that I was lost for something to say. How could mere words about God make sense to a man in such agony? I sat in confusion for several seconds.

'Max?' Dave's longing for consolation loosened my tongue.

'God does care, Dave,' I began hesitantly. Was I only going to manage to speak in cliches? Dear Lord, help me to understand and find wisdom to speak.

152

'I . . . can't say I always know why God allows things. I think we just have to trust Him, trust that He's looking after us even in the bad times.'

Dave groaned, as if he didn't think much of my answer.

'It's because I've experienced God's love for me, and seen the good things He does, that I can trust Him,' I tried to explain.

Dave's eyes were closed. He didn't respond. I could only pray that somehow, God would help him understand.

It was so easy to feel like blaming God for difficulty and pain. Even I found myself questioning deep inside, faced with suffering like Dave's. But remembering just one of God's promises, made through Paul in his letter to the Romans, brought reassurance: 'We know that in everything God works for good with those who love him, who are called according to his purpose.'

But Dave had never consciously experienced God's love, or learnt to love Him in return. No wonder he found it impossible to see beyond his immediate pain. How could I explain that he was the object of a battle between Satan and God, as we all were, that only because evil came into God's created world was suffering any part of it now? How could I assure him of God's omnipotence, even with Satan in among His people?

I couldn't tell whether Dave was sleeping, thinking, or perhaps praying. If he was really seeking to understand, I knew he would find something.

One thing was becoming clearer in my mind. The more things went well the more we carried on in our own way, unconcerned about where God came into it. But if something happened to thwart us, like an accident which reduced us to complete dependence, some of the barriers against God were broken down. We could no longer pretend we could manage on our own.

So perhaps one of the reasons God allowed trials was to draw us closer to Him, to remind us of our true relation to Him: children dependent on the Father. Pain wasn't evidence of God's absence, but a sign that He cared.

Day after day in the physiotherapy department, Ebba teased and cajoled, bullied and encouraged me to push on with every conceivable exercise. She was fast becoming a good friend. Her total acceptance of disability as being something as natural as brushing your teeth every day was one of the keys to her quiet brilliance at her job. She wasn't intense, neither did she have the give-away, over-sympathetic approach to me which marked out the people who found my handicap awkward. Her easy, matter-of-fact manner bolstered my confidence, helped me to come to terms with my situation.

It was in the hydrotherapy pool that I'd first supported myself upright on my own. Standing between two waist-high parallel bars beneath the surface of the water, I'd clung to them so that most of my weight was supported by my tense and trembling arms.

In the physio department, back on dry land, Ebba wasn't content to have me merely standing between the bars. She wanted me to walk.

'Now Max, don't be lazy,' she chided, refusing to see the look of petrified disbelief on my face. 'Lean forward a little, and swing from your hip.'

I had confidence in Ebba's judgment by now. If she thought I could manage something, I probably could, but it was only after I'd taken my first uncertain step and collapsed laughing against Ebba, waiting to catch me, that I believed it myself.

Our sessions were constant mixtures of elation and frustration, laughter and tears. If Ebba thought I wasn't working hard enough, she would start hobbling round the room, imitating me, complete with dead-pan serious expression. Sometimes she'd burst into giggles before I got round to hurling a pillow in her direction. Invariably she was right in detecting some lazy habit, and I would marvel at her having got to know me so well. Because I was sure of her genuine understanding of my fears and up-and-down feelings, I didn't mind the fun she made of me. All the laughter must have been great for strengthening my stomach muscles!

Early in December, rumour of a royal visit flew excitedly round the hospital.

'The Duchess of Kent is coming,' confirmed Sister Clements. 'So you'll all have to be on your best behaviour.'

Much scrubbing and polishing, arranging and rearranging went on in preparation for this great occasion. We all maintained the Duchess was coming to check up on the staff.

'Make sure you treat us properly on the day,' we delighted in warning our long-suffering nurses. And 'You won't get away with that when the Duchess is here,' was a frequent contribution from Dave Pembury when one of the staff didn't comply with his wishes.

The day dawned at last, and to all appearances 2X was a calm, civilised ward with never a raised voice or a cross word. The Duchess of Kent, smiling and with an appropriate word for everyone, graciously made her way round the ward until she reached me. Dr. Maynard introduced me by name, and the Duchess held out her hand.

'How do you do?' she said warmly.

'May I stand to shake your hand,' I blurted out before I lost my nerve. From the moment I knew she'd arrived, I'd determined to stand up to greet her.

'Please do,' the Duchess sounded delighted, and stood patiently while I struggled to my feet. Somewhat unsteadily, I grasped her hand.

'Mr. Sinclair is doing well,' Dr. Maynard filled in the pause unexpectedly, leaning confidentially towards the Duchess. 'He'll walk again.'

I was so astonished I almost lost my balance completely.

'Do . . . do you really mean that?' I gasped. It was the first time anyone had ever said it.

'Yes indeed.'

I caught the Duchess' eye. It was twinkling with merriment. Together we burst out laughing, she in delight at sharing the news and I in amazed joy.

155

The parallel bars gave way to short bursts of my pushing my wheelchair ahead of me, taking two, three and then more wobbly steps. Ebba stood in front of the mirror in the physio department and made me watch my hopelessly unco-ordinated movements, then proceeded to drill me in deportment.

'Head high, shoulders back, and don't cheat by dragging that right foot. Get a good swing from your hip.'

As I became stronger I found myself feeling embarrassed and almost guilty when I was with my fellow-patients. I sometimes noticed looks of silent sadness in the eyes of those who had arrived in hospital when I did, and yet were still confined to their beds or, at best, a wheelchair. I became particularly self-conscious one night when we were all sitting watching Top of the Pops.

'Max, old man,' someone addressed me halfway through. 'Would you mind not tapping your feet?' He tried to bring an apologetic laugh into his voice, but there was no disguising the deep feeling which had prompted the words. I had been doing it completely unconsciously, without even realising how fortunate I was to be able to tap my feet at all. Most of those around me would never experience that simple pleasure again.

It didn't seem fair, when others had tried harder than me and with more determination. All of a sudden we weren't quite running the race together any more.

I was careful not to practise my walking in the ward, not to offer my help too often. From my own experience I knew it was easier to accept help from the staff. It was their job to do things the patients couldn't manage, whereas if friends or family proffered help it only seemed to intensify the predicament.

On the other hand, there were several things Dave Pembury or one of the others could do from their wheelchairs that I always had difficulty with. Dave was excellent at cutting up my meat, or doing up a button that had come undone, and could beat me hands down at table tennis. On such occasions, our comradeship seemed back on its old footing.

Sometimes, the tragedy we'd all suffered in one way or another broke through the surface bravery and cheerfulness. Tommy, a great rugby enthusiast before his accident, related a dream he'd had in which he'd wheeled himself across a rugby pitch to where a match was in play. He'd jumped out of his chair and joined in, scoring a hard-won try before clambering back into his wheelchair and leaving the game behind.

'How do you think I got the idea into my head of playing rugby when I was still in my wheelchair?' Tommy had laughed at the craziness of his dream, but the longing behind it was all too apparent.

And Terry, a young teenager who'd never seemed to worry about what the future held, asked us all one day what car he should buy with his compensation money so he could drive himself off a cliff and commit suicide.

Many, many times I longed for the others to find the resource of faith in God's plan that I drew from. Life wouldn't be bearable for me without it.

I could now get myself to the hospital chapel for services, and at any time when I felt in need of some quiet moments in prayer. I always found it helpful to be in God's appointed house when it came to praying. I could focus my thoughts better, and prayer became deep and meaningful. No matter how good my intentions to pray regularly in normal, everyday situations, I rarely achieved that close communion with God I experienced in His chapel. There were too many distractions in the busy Stoke Mandeville world.

So the little hospital chapel became a place of refuge, of personal encounter with God. It was a hut all to itself, standing proudly near the entrance gates. Inside it seemed like a missionary hut with high church intentions. It was whitewashed and stark, but on the table that served as an altar there were two heavily ornate candlesticks. Hard, high-backed chairs were ranged down the left side, while the right was left clear to accommodate wheelchairs and perhaps a bed or two. The services were simple and quite formal, but every moment was special to me. Only when something is denied you do you realise its value. I'd really missed being able to attend a church service.

God was continuing to answer prayer in the most wonderful way.

Christmas was drawing closer when the subject of my ultimate discharge from Stoke came up. Depending on how well I coped at home over the Christmas period, the doctors felt I could probably leave towards the end of January.

A whole mixture of feelings tumbled through me. Relief and gratitude mixed with apprehension, regret at the thought of losing my new friends, and wonder that I'd actually recovered far beyond any original expectation. One moment the single month that remained for me at Stoke seemed far too long, and the next it seemed no time at all. There was still so much I wanted to do before I braved the outside world.

One of the activities we'd been looking forward to for a long time was a Christmas trip to hear a performance of the Messiah at the Royal Albert Hall in London. I'd even wheeled myself to the hospital library and found a dusty copy of Handel's score to peruse in preparation for the evening. We were all as excited as schoolboys as about a dozen of us piled into assorted cars for the trip.

London was as full of noise and life as I remembered. So much colour and festivity. But the fun abruptly died out of us once the car doors were open and we were struggling out into our wheelchairs. Then the streams of people on the pavement seemed hostile as they stared at us, the noise of the traffic drowned our voices and the bright lights only exposed our helplessness the more.

Penny pushed me along the bumpy pavement, right to the front of the queue of people waiting for tickets. I could feel the stares prickling the back of my neck. It was one of those occasions I could have wished the floor would open up and swallow me. Inside, we had to disturb the people in the foyer to get to the lift, and only when the lights went down and we were invisible could I relax.

The performance lived up to all our expectations. It was a feast of sound, a triumph of praise. I couldn't remember ever having heard anything so beautiful.

At the end of the evening we were vulnerable to curious faces and pitying looks once again. In the bewildering stampede of people rushing to leave the Hall I felt like putting my hands over my face for protection. It was my first real taste of the humiliating stigma of the wheelchair.

Christmas was upon us very quickly, and I spent ten days at home. We had lots of visitors, and I had to manoeuvre my chair through all sort of tricky situations. There was more time to adapt than on a weekend, and I found myself appreciating all the good things about being at home rather than feeling bowed down by the difficulties. At the end of it all, I didn't want to come back to Stoke – the first time I'd felt that way.

'Won't be long,' Sue said cheerfully when she left me looking rather downcast back in 2X. 'Make the most of the last few weeks.'

It was wise advice, and I didn't find it at all difficult to follow once I was back in the swing of the hospital routine. The days flew by.

'A last race then, Max?' challenged Tommy when it was formally announced that I'd be leaving Stoke on 20th January, exactly six months to the day after my accident.

'You're on.'

There was a stretch of corridor which sloped beautifully, making an ideal track for racing wheelchairs. Many a grand prix had taken place there, with the participants dicing with death at terrifying speeds.

Tommy and I lined up in the starting position, and launched ourselves off down the incline. I was just reaching my maximum speed, when the fate we'd all successfully avoided on previous occasions befell me. One of the office doors opened and the Senior Medical Social Worker ventured out on to the race track. She held a kettle in one hand, and was obviously looking forward to a cup of coffee.

The next few seconds saw a dramatic change in the Social Worker's demeanour. Her smile transformed itself to a look of horror, and she began a series of little hopping movements from side to side as if she was attempting some kind of dance. Lamenting the fact that Social Workers chose to do their dancing practice during race meetings, I had no choice but to employ the wheelchair equivalent of an emergency stop. I jammed on first one brake and then the other, swinging myself alarmingly from side to side across the corridor and causing even more frenzied dancing from the Social Worker.

Only when my speeding vehicle made contact with the unfortunate Social Worker's ankles, knocking her gracefully into a heap on my lap, did I finally come to a halt. Now I'd well and truly lost the race. Tommy sped past to the finishing point as I tried to apologise to a bewildered Social Worker, struggling to her feet with the kettle still clutched in one hand.

For my final week at the hospital I was transferred to Ashendon House, the hostel Sue stayed in when I was first brought to Stoke. It served as a rehabilitation hostel as well as a place for visitors. I had to walk pushing my wheelchair for ten minutes across rather icy pavements to reach my new, temporary abode, and I went in constant fear of falling flat on my face and displaying my handicap to anyone who might be passing. I tried hard to remember all that Ebba had taught me in front of the mirror in the physio department, but I knew my movements were still stiff and ungainly. It was a relief when I reached the safety of the door and could hide myself inside.

The corridors were quiet, dimly-lit. As I wheeled myself along, looking for my room, I thought of Susie spending night after night in this lonely place while I was in intensive care at the hospital. How hard it must have been for her. And how amazing that she didn't just 'cope' but was filled with a smiling joy that shone from her eyes and overflowed to me and many others. God had worked a miracle in her life as He had in mine.

My room looked comfortable, but bare. My personal belongings were packed into two plastic bags, and it didn't take long for me to arrange everything neatly in the drawers and cupboard. Then I just sat motionless in my wheelchair, awed by the silence. I'd been with people continually for six whole months. This was my first real privacy. I felt the same mixture of excitement and fear I remembered feeling at eighteen, when I'd left the farm to lead my own life at University. Here I was, on the threshold of independence after so long, yet about to lose the precious security of the hospital. It was a strange feeling.

In response to a long-denied instinct, I pulled myself out of my wheelchair and down on to my knees beside the bed. It gave me a tremendous thrill to be able to express physically again my submission and gratitude to God. In that attitude I began to pray, conscious of the need to commit the uncertain future to God once more. In the quietness of that room, with nothing to distract or interrupt me, I found myself pouring out my whole heart to God. My regrets, my fears, my joy and sorrows – it all tumbled out. And not just that evening, but the next and the next. I felt broken and weak, conscious that I was no less vulnerable to temptation than I had been before the accident and afraid that I might give in to the difficulties at home and forget the many blessings of the past six months.

God answered by directing me to significant passages in Scripture. As if He'd written them specially for me, they met my need for reassurance and hope.

> 'Thou dost keep him in perfect peace,
>     whose mind is stayed on thee,
>     because he trusts in thee.
> Trust in the Lord for ever,
>     for the Lord God
>     is an everlasting rock.'

Isaiah 26:3, 4

That was so simple, yet the key to my present turmoil. Here was God promising, not that my problems would go away, but that He would cope with them for me if I allowed Him to. He was the ultimate source of total security, the solid rock to which I should be anchored. Once I grasped that, my mind would be filled with peace, not worry.

'This precious treasure – this light and power that now shine within us – is held in a perishable container, that is, in our weak bodies. Everyone can see that the glorious power within must be from God and is not our own.'

2 Corinthians 4:6, 7 (Living Bible)

At first, it was hard to appreciate that God seemed to be saying my weakness was actually an advantage. It allowed God to show Himself even more powerfully and beautifully. But gradually that made sense to me, and even thrilled me. The picture of the flowers on the hospital rubbish dump came to mind again, and thankfulness overtook my apprehension. How could I be afraid when there was God's continuing handiwork to look forward to?

I couldn't help feeling subdued as the last day dawned. Now I would have to say the goodbyes I'd been dreading. Of course I'd come back, perhaps for a check up or just to visit old friends, but it wouldn't be the same. I had noticed the change in my own attitude towards the patients who returned for quick visits. Somehow they were different. They'd become outsiders simply because they'd begun a new life in another world. They were not rejected or resented, but inevitably the relationship had changed. I knew I'd be saying goodbye to the unique and precious 'fellowship of suffering' I'd enjoyed in 2X.

It seemed the others felt something was being lost too. Boyd put it into words over breakfast, in one of his famous announcements.

'Can everyone 'ear me?' he bawled in his thick, Brighton accent. Our cornflakes all but jumped out of their bowls at the volume of this demand.

'I 'ave something very important to say, so I 'ope yer all listening.' We were dutifully quiet. 'I am very sad,' Boyd continued gravely. 'Today is a sad day. Max is leaving us. This is the beginning of the end.'

A hush followed this infallible pronouncement as if more wise words were expected of our sage, but nothing further transpired. Subdued, everyone went on with their cornflakes.

I went for my physio session as usual, partly because I wanted to loosen up for the day, and partly because I couldn't miss saying goodbye to Ebba, however difficult that would be.

After I'd been through my exercises to her satisfaction, she disappeared for a moment to find the list of tasks she'd devised for me to practise at home. I'd known I might receive such a document, and had been half-dreading its appearance because of its confirmation that the next stage would be up to me alone.

But when I saw what Ebba had prepared, my dread melted into amusement and heartfelt gratitude. The heading was 'Maxes latest party trix', and underneath, in coded Swedish spelling, were my orders. 'Passiv Sid Stretch' was one. 'Stretch Tendon Achilles' another. 'Sit from Sid to Sid' came half way down the list, and also a reference to assiduously practising my 'pretty walking'. Little illustrations appeared every so often to help my understanding, and at the bottom, in true Ebba-style, were the words, 'Have a nice time. Don't cheat.'

I looked up at her smiling satisfaction before her work of art with a lump in my throat. Ebba had taken the trouble to think something out which was specially suited to motivating me. All her lighthearted but practical character was there. In a way she'd still be working with me as I went through her exercises on my own.

My final call of the morning was the chapel. Canon Byard had asked me if I'd like a brief Communion service all to myself, a last opportunity to thank God with him before I left Stoke.

Sue was expected for lunch with a special farewell treat for all the hungry mouths in the ward. At twelve o'clock I was looking out anxiously for her, and at last the car swung through the hospital gates and pulled up outside the French windows. Susie emerged with huge trifles and mousses, bowls of fruit salad and cream, to the astonishment and delight of my colleagues in 2X. There wasn't much demand for the usual national health service approved arctic roll that day.

More painful farewells and stumbling attempts at thanks to the staff, then I was in the car waving to those who could get to the French windows. As we left the hospital behind, I caught Susie's eye.

'Hallelujah,' we exclaimed together.

# CHAPTER 11

'How long are you staying this time, Daddy?' It was Noddy, looking quizzically at me over a large mug of milk.

'For ever and ever,' I sang. 'I don't have to go back to the hospital any more.'

'Oh good.' Noddy beamed, lowered her eyes and went back to the serious task of drinking her milk.

The children weren't the only ones finding it hard to get used to my being at home permanently after so long. I still had to remind myself that I'd be waking every morning in my own bed from now on, that there'd be no orderly brandishing a brightly-coloured flannel to ensure I really had left dreamland behind, that I could choose how to spend the day rather than have to keep to a strict hospital routine. It was all rather heady at first.

'Breakfast in bed, Max, or down with the children?' Sue would ask after we'd shared our Bible reading for the day and prayed together. The simple joy of doing that again after six months filled us both with delight. Irrepressible grins would creep to our lips, and at the least provocation we'd be laughing merrily like two newly-weds. In prayer, I could feel the bridges being built again after our long separation. Which was a comfort, because during the busy days, each of us preoccupied with different things, it was less easy to draw close.

'In bed,' I tended to answer. Or, 'I'll come down later to eat.' It took me so long to wash, dress and propel myself downstairs, I preferred the family to rush on at its own pace without having to wait for me. Sue had to help me with my wheelchair as well, and there were always more than enough demands on her time with getting the girls off to school and Benjy ready for the day. No, it was better that I stayed quietly in bed until later.

Then I'd be stricken with the responsibility of how I was going to divide my time that day. Physiotherapy and letter-writing would come into it somewhere, but there was no hurry for either to be done first thing. Some reading perhaps. Or, another hour's sleep to give me maximum strength and energy for whatever I decided upon.

It was funny how the day actually took on a more daunting aspect at home than it had done at Stoke. It was one thing not to have to face the rigorous demands of the physio and occupational therapy departments, but quite another to have to motivate myself to save the day from waste. I began to see how the routine of the hospital had actually made life easier. I had goals to achieve, and chivying nurses and therapists to make sure I got down to work. At home, there was no pattern to follow, and it was all too easy to become lazy. The luxury of time to think turned me into myself again, brought troubled reflections on how little I could manage and allowed the old demon of self-pity to sap my confidence and energy.

How odd to feel hospital-sick! I was surprised at how

much I missed my friends and the bustling activity of the ward.

I had to establish my own routine. Grabbing my old friends pencil and paper again, I set out to write down an order for each day. Physiotherapy, following Ebba's thoughtful instructions, from nine to ten, then coffee break with Sue in the kitchen. Then letter-writing from ten thirty to eleven thirty, perhaps longer if I wasn't too exhausted. At least I could keep in touch with Tommy and Boyd and the others by letter. And there were still lots of 'thank you' notes to write to all those I knew were continuing to pray for us. A choice in the afternoons: perhaps a walk with Susie and Sunny dog to the end of the garden, or a game with Ben. Some quiet reading, and then later, when the girls came in from school, time to be with them and help with homework.

I felt better when I'd filled a sheet of paper with my spidery left-handed writing. There was lots to do.

And of course almost every day someone came round to visit us, wanting to congratulate me on being home at last and to fill me in on the latest news. On more than one occasion, I was in the middle of Ebba's 'Passiv Sid Stretch' or 'Sit from Sid to Sid' when an old friend was announced and I'd find myself staring up from my prostrate position on the floor into an astonished or curious face.

At home, where I should have been more at my ease with visitors, I found myself less so. Self-conscious, and aware of what I used to be, it was difficult to relax unless I could sense the other person understood my situation. Which wasn't often. I laboured under a devastating sense of isolation, probably quite disproportionate but nonetheless very real to me. None of these people had been through my experience of the last six months, and I couldn't believe they really understood. I just saw the looks of sympathy – or worse, pity – which only seemed to seal my aloneness. Oh for the hospital where wheelchairs were accepted and handicap was normal.

To my horror and wretchedness, I even felt cut off from Susie. She tried to understand, and I knew she did for the most part, but there was always a point beyond which her insight didn't extend. Only now I was back at home did I realise how much of the Stoke Mandeville experience she'd missed and how she couldn't be expected to know how I felt in my wheelchair. Of course she couldn't fully appreciate the magnitude of my scratching my hand without noticing any pain, or the humiliation of her having to carry my wheelchair up and down stairs while I painfully and slowly dragged myself over the steps on my behind. She was full of gladness and love at having me back, and being with her again was like a second honeymoon, but niggling underneath was that sickening sense of isolation. Now I wished more than ever we'd had some privacy to talk and share at the hospital. But we never did. There were always others around, and I'd never been able to convey to my best friend what one of the most important experiences of my life was really all about.

It didn't matter at first, and I told myself time would help anyway. But weeks after I'd come home, I would still watch with burning resentment Susie's figure running down the garden to pick strawberries or dig in the vegetable patch. I envied the activity which was for ever denied me.

'Daddy's a sitting down person and Mummy's a running about person', Noddy had said with surprising perception long before the accident. Now this was even more the case, and somehow I had to learn to accept it and come to terms with it.

And Ben still didn't really understand who I was. His childish looks of mistrust cut me to the core. For a long time he called me 'chair', the most identifiable part for him of this strange package that had invaded his home. I think it was a year after my discharge from hospital that he volunteered his first concrete sign of affection. I'd been mowing the lawn, and had lain down to rest on the sweet-smelling grass. Ben toddled up and sat himself on my chest.

'Daddy, you're my friend. I like you.'

That was a celebration day.

Naomi and Anna accepted me again almost as if I'd

never been away. That meant a lot to me, and many a time I was overcome with a mixture of gratitude and great tenderness towards them. Until they expected something of me that I could no longer manage. The first school morning of my being at home, Annie came softly, barefoot up to my bed as she always used to and turned her back for me to fasten her dress. She didn't need to ask me to do it, for it was a ritual we both knew too well by now. Normally, I'd zip or button away, and she'd skip out of the room.

That morning, she stood patiently while I fumbled with the zip on her dress. She said nothing as the seconds ticked away, and her obvious trust that I could manage even if it took a little longer made me want to cry with frustration. I couldn't do it.

'Annie love, I'm afraid I can't do you up. I should go and ask Mummy.' Dutifully she padded out, apparently accepting this change in routine like a change in the weather – something that just happened. But I felt crushingly useless.

It was Annie who taught me an important lesson when I'd been at home some time and yet still couldn't quite accept the loss of my original role. One evening at bedtime, indulging in the usual childish distractions to prolong the moment before the light finally went out, Annie suddenly became serious.

'Do you remember how you used to carry me 'round, Daddy?'

'Well, yes I do,' I replied hesitantly, wondering whether this was just a new ploy to keep me from my firm 'good night'.

'At bedtime you used to carry me all round upstairs just for fun. We pretended not to know where my bedroom was, didn't we?'

'Yes,' I said bleakly. The scenes were alive in my memory. She was wriggling in my arms, laughing delightedly. 'No, not this one Daddy!' at every dark room we peered into, and a final peal of protest when I threatened to put her to bed in the bath.

'That was before your accident, wasn't it, Daddy?' The

comment, serious though it was, was a simple statement of fact. 'It was fun, wasn't it?'

'Yes,' I murmured, torn between regret and hurt and unsure whether Annie was grieved that I couldn't play with her like this any more.

'Do you mind that we don't do that now?' I ventured.

Her freckled face took on a little grinning, twinkling look. 'Don't be so silly, Daddy. I was a little baby then. You couldn't carry me now any way.'

There was a corrective tone in her voice, and I found myself grinning stupidly at this matter-of-fact reassurance.

'Do you know what else I remember, Daddy?'

'Tell me,' I said, trying to sound casual when really I was elated with relief. Here was my daughter remembering happy times of the past without any hint of regret that the present was different. Thank the Lord there was no harbouring unhappiness in her from the traumatic days of the accident. And if she accepted me so easily as I was now, what was stopping me from doing so?

'I remember your monstrous bed in hospital,' Annie continued with satisfaction. 'It was so monstrous Noddy and I could sit on it beside you when you were lying down. And I remember Tommy and Boyd. I used to go and talk to them didn't I?' She paused for my approval. How easily the hospital could have been a nightmare for her, but she chatted on with obvious enjoyment as she remembered one thing after another. I forgot to be firm and turn out the light until a huge yawn interrupted her discourse.

I gradually got used to manoeuvring my wheelchair round the house. I walked tentatively with a stick and a lot of help from Susie, and felt my confidence returning. Then something would happen to remind me brutally of the reality of my helplessness. One day I was sitting reading in the living room and found myself getter colder and colder as I often did when I wasn't moving about. The phone had just rung in the kitchen, and I could hear Susie chatting through the closed door. I wondered whether to wait until she was finished to ask her to turn on the fan heater, but decided I might as well do it myself. There was no reason why I couldn't manage that simple job.

I hauled myself off the sofa and balanced myself upright with my stick. A couple of wobbly steps brought me to the little squat heater, and with masterful ingenuity I kicked the the 'on' button. Nothing happened, and I realised the thing wasn't plugged in. We were always careful to disconnect our electrical appliances at Pepperland because of the danger of fire. Determined now not to admit defeat, I opened the door into the kitchen to reach the nearest socket, and bent down to pick up the plug. The next thing I knew was my back had crumpled and I was falling heavily forward to the sound of a horrified scream from Susie.

'Max, Max what are you doing? Are you all right? What happened, what happened?' The phone hung crazily down from the table where she'd dropped it, and my head span.

'I'm fine,' I mumbled, furious and frightened, sick at the thought that I might have damaged my neck again. The fact that no harm was done gave me little consolation. I was still horribily vulnerable.

And the day that Ben fell downstairs. He could hardly manage them really, and made his way up and down by a funny combination of crawling and sitting and climbing. I was wheeling myself slowly past the bottom of the stairs in my wheelchair and looked up in time to see Ben try to step down from the top landing as he'd seen others do. In slow motion, with the yell of warning stuck in my throat, I watched his little leg fail to reach solid ground and his body topple. Instinctively, I tried to lurch out of my chair to catch him, but I couldn't move fast enough. He bounced, arms flailing, like a rag doll down to my feet. I couldn't even bend to pick him up as his screams brought Susie running.

What sort of father could I be now? If my own son could almost kill himself before my very eyes. The hurt and isolation and fright knotted itself up inside me until I wondered how I would carry on.

Then we heard that the BBC radio programme, 'Woman's

Hour' wanted to record a ten minute interview with us about the accident and its effects.

'Really?' Sue was incredulous as Pam delivered the news. Pam Gillham was a long standing friend and freelance radio broadcaster. She'd been greatly impressed by the way God had upheld us through the months of uncertainty and trauma after the accident, and had approached the producer of 'Woman's Hour' with the idea of an interview.

'I knew she'd be interested,' Pam told us. 'Your story is a must for broadcast. Of course there'll be a small fee.'

Sue's expression changed to one of doubt, and she cast an uneasy glance across to me. Pam laughted delightedly. 'No – *you* won't have to pay,' she reassured my frugal Susie. 'The BBC will pay *you*!' We obviously needed educating in the world of broadcasting.

Here was our first opportunity to share with millions what God had done for us. We were breathless with excitement and nerves as Pam set up the tape recorder and ran over a few possible questions she wanted to put to us. In our own front room, it wasn't difficult to recall details of the past few months with Pam's expert encouragement, and as I relived the experiences I found myself overwhelmed again with the love God had shown us. My frustrations of the present paled beside the undeniable fact of my recovery, the wonder of the solid-as-concrete presence of God beside me through the crisis, the real support He had given Susie and the children when they needed it.

'And why do you think God let this happen to you?' Pam asked finally. I knew there wasn't time for me to express at length all that I'd learnt about asking 'Why?' of God, so I tried to put it as succinctly as possible. My conversation with Dave Pembury came back to me as I spoke.

'God doesn't say life will be problem-free. Nowhere in the Bible will you find that,' I emphasised. 'It's what you do with your problems that counts. Somehow we must have faith in God's purpose, knowing that any difficulty will be there for a reason and we can learn from it.' Even as I spoke, I knew that I myself needed reminding of this: my problems adjusting at home were no different from the more serious crisis in this respect. Turned over to Him, they would cease to have a hold.

The response to the programme when it was broadcast was overwhelming. People wrote in, grateful for the encouragement our story had given them, eager to hear more or to share their own experiences. Some spoke of a specific need met by something Sue or I had said which related to their situation, and for the first time I appreciated how our testimony could be a help to those in any kind of need. It wasn't only relevant to those who'd had critical accidents. God was concerned about any trouble, small or large, and could intervene for anyone as He had for us.

A new understanding grew within me as these appreciative letters reached us. Here was God bringing something very positive out of the accident, definite 'rubbish dump flowers' which revived my hope in the usefulness of my disabled life.

Gradually, this 'new ministry' was made clearer by God. A phone call on the recommendation of her vicar brought Judy Ridgeway round to see me. Her brother had been in a serious motor bike accident and was now in hospital, and Judy couldn't accept that a loving God had allowed this. Her fears and resentments tumbled out in a rush as we sat over a cup of tea, and I tried again to explain that we could only trust in God's purposes, however difficult they might be to understand. She listened and nodded, and I felt that if I hadn't been sitting in my wheelchair with my own experience behind me she would never have come to see me in the first place let alone been able to take seriously what I said.

It was the same with the young teacher who'd lost her father a year before and still couldn't come to terms with the loss. I was able to share how difficult I found it even months after the accident to accept the 'loss' of my body, and she took consolation from the fact that she wasn't alone in her feelings.

'It does help to have someone to talk to who really

understands,' she said warmly before leaving. It flashed across my mind that I wouldn't have been able to offer that consolation if I'd been standing fully healed before her. Was this perhaps a hint of why God had allowed only limited recovery? I reflected on the fact that it was easier for people to identify with the sort of trauma I'd been through if they could *see* I'd been through it. It is always a thrill to catch a glimpse of God's purpose, and I was thrilled then as I saw how my weakness could actually be a strength.

Requests for me to speak to various groups and Christian Unions began to trickle in. At first I was very reluctant. All sorts of possible complications filled me with dread, and the thought of being exposed to dozens of strange pairs of eyes made me want to curl up and hide.

'Max, it won't be like that,' Sue tried to encourage me. 'They really want to hear what you have to say, otherwise they wouldn't have invited you. They won't be hostile.'

She was right of course, but my lack of courage prevailed over my contrary desire to share what God had done, until Sue found a date in the diary that had already been booked for me to speak and I couldn't get out of it. It had been arranged before the accident, and strangely enough was entitled 'The Purpose of Suffering'. I think I'd even prepared some rough notes when I was first asked if I'd talk on that topic.

How could I wave this aside? Now I was uniquely qualified to talk about suffering. If this wasn't a nudge from God to get on and do it I don't know what was.

I went. I almost forgot about my handicap as I answered the many heartfelt questions that resulted from my brief talk about what I'd learnt about suffering. Encouraged, I accepted more engagements, and always there were seeking, soul-searching questions.

Do you think your accident was punishment from God?' The serious, thin-faced enquirer looked searchingly at me from the back of the hall.

I thought carefully before I responded, and the intense voice spoke up again.

'You see I had a serious car accident a while ago, and one of my religious friends told me he thought it was a punishment.'

'Well,' I began. 'Speaking for myself I know I've certainly done quite enough to deserve God's punishment. We're all in the same boat there. But of course the point of Christ coming into the world was to take our sins on Himself and suffer the punishment for us.' I remembered that Jesus Himself had been asked a similar question, and recounted the story from the Bible of the man born blind. 'Who sinned, this man or his parents, that he was born blind?' the disciples questioned. Jesus replied that his blindness was not because of anyone's sin, but because God wanted to do something special in his life. That 'something special' was the miraculous cure of his blindness.

'And today it could be any number of things for any one of us,' I finished, hoping the men in front of me understood. 'Affliction gives God the opportunity to do something special for us.'

Of the 'special somethings' Sue and I were continually witnessing, one of the most welcome and touching was the support of friends, Christian or otherwise. We very much wanted to do something in return for the many kindnesses we'd been shown, and after some discussion hit on the idea of an 'At Home' evening.

'Then we'd have a chance to share some of the things we've learnt too,' Susie enthused. Both of us were thrilled by the increasing number of opportunities to tell others about God's bounty to us. It was too good to keep to ourselves, and we wanted our friends to know they could experience His love too.

So we dished out invitations and Sue concocted a mouth-watering array of food, enough to feed an army. I donned my best suit for the occasion, trimmed my beard and tried my hardest to banish any self-consciousness.

The first person to walk through the door was none other than Colin Morrison, who'd trained with me in Accountancy. I'd prayed with all my heart and soul for him to come

174

to know the Lord, and I'd never forgotten the day he took his step of faith. Now he was here, embracing me and marvelling how his own prayers for me had been answered. At that moment I really knew what it meant to be part of God's whole family.

The evening went like a dream, everyone listening seriously to the speaker we'd invited to say a few words about a passage of Scripture. At the end there were the searching questions I had now come to expect, and our guests left with warm thanks and thoughtful faces.

'You ought to do that more often,' Pam told us when she phoned with her own personal 'thank you' for encouraging her to look more seriously to God. 'People really appreciated hearing what you had to say, you know,' she continued. 'Why don't you think of having some kind of study or discussion evening on a regular basis?'

The seed was sown. We tossed the idea about between us, and eventually decided we couldn't waste such an opportunity. A Bible study in a firelit sitting room with coffee and plenty of time to discuss whatever needed working through – there *was* a need for that in our middle class, self-sufficient area, where people tended to keep any serious, troubling questions out of sight and rarely thought of discussing them during the normal course of things.

'It's worth a try,' Sue echoed my thoughts as we came to a decision. 'You never know – this might be another flower on the rubbish dump.'

We were amazed at the number of people who came to our first Bible study, and who came again the next time. Pam caught my eye during a particularly heated discussion at one point, and grinned knowingly. She'd been right. God was showing us another new area of ministry, which we wouldn't have thought about if it wasn't for the accident.

A phone call from Penny back at Stoke brought a further opportunity.

'You know you said we might come over and stay any time. . .' she said once we'd finished sharing all our news. 'Well, I wondered if I could bring John and Sandra one

175

weekend. John is much better now, and they could both do with a break from Stoke. . .'

'Yes, yes of course,' I almost shouted with excitement. To see some Stoke friends again would be marvellous, especially John. He'd arrived at the hospital towards the end of my stay, and although we had little in common we soon developed a firm friendship. 'As unlike as chalk and cheese', Boyd used to say of Dave Pembury and myself. 'Can't understand how you two get on.' It was the same for John and me. Stoke provided a unique opportunity for us to get to know each other, an opportunity we wouldn't have had otherwise.

'Come whenever you like, as soon as you can.'

The trio invaded Pepperland the following weekend.

'Eh Sinclair, it's good to see you again. You look just the same. And wot a fabulous place you 'ave 'ere.' John and his pretty wife Sandra exclaimed wide-eyed at the beautiful countryside, our log fire and Susie's home baking. Coming from inner London, they didn't often experience wide open spaces and peace and quiet.

Penny looked critically at my walk, as I tried desperately not to seem too stiff.

'Your leg's dragging a bit,' she said. 'Can't you pick it up better? Could do with straightening your back too.'

I grinned at this warm-hearted scolding, delighted to be given some of the old Stoke Mandeville treatment. I knew I hadn't concentrated on Ebba's exercises as much as I should but 'I don't have the same incentive working on my own,' I told Penny in defence.

'No excuse,' she replied, which made me grin even more.

'I still wonder why God let me live, Max,' John said out of the blue as we all relaxed that evening, having exhausted ourselves with hilarious reminiscences of 2X.

John had been seriously injured in a car accident down at the docks where he'd worked all his life. Sandra had been given little hope he would survive, and in desperation had gone to the hospital chapel to pray – something she hadn't done for a long time.

'And God answered me, John,' I heard her telling a baffled husband when he was well enough to understand. 'You started to get better the day after I prayed.'

John was as struck by this as Sandra had been, and although he didn't open his heart at once to God as his wife had done in her relief and gratitude, he started searching and questioning.

'Why do you think 'e let me live, Max?'

I could see Sandra looking at me anxiously.

'Did you think much about God before your accident?' I asked.

'No – not much. You know 'ow it is when you've got lots of other things to think about.'

'Well – maybe God wanted you to think about Him.' A phrase of St. Augustine came to mind: God wants to give us something, but cannot, because our hands are full – there's nowhere for Him to put it. 'Perhaps your hands were so full God had to take everything away rather dramatically before you could understand that real happiness can only be found through sharing your life with Him. Now He's giving you a second chance.'

'To make my life more useful,' John said thoughtfully. 'Yeah, that makes sense.'

More and more questions came up over the weekend, and when the time came to return to Stoke, John and Sandra were radiant with new understanding.

'Amazing, Max. Just amazing,' John repeated endlessly.

I watched the car disappear down the drive with regret. The last thing Penny had said to me was 'Keep practising your walking', but I still doubted my ability to make much real headway on my own. But God had that in hand too. Shortly afterwards, Sue was on the phone to Penny, making a very special request.

It all began when Justyn came over from the Hall one day, looking haggard and almost ill with exhaustion. He'd carried the can for too long.

'I don't think I can continue, Max,' he said. 'I need to get away for a bit.'

And God had allowed me to recover sufficiently to step in, much as Justyn had stepped in for me all those months ago. Or so I thought. I'd already spoken at the Hall a few times since coming home, to delighted audiences of those who'd prayed for my recovery, and it didn't take much for me to throw myself into all the administration once again.

For a while, I managed to put in the necessary hours, speak at the conferences, and even travel short distances with my hard-won, left-footed driving ability. But it didn't last. Physical and mental exhaustion drained my few resources. I knew I was trying to continue as before, as if I hadn't been in a car crash and broken my neck, as if I wasn't limited to a wheelchair most of the time and still on drugs to cope with my spasticity.

I was needed. My days were full again. I didn't want to admit defeat. How could I let down all the trustees, the loyal staff, those who were praying? Surely God hadn't brought me this far to let me fall again. But I simply could not fulfil all the demands made on me.

That was when Sue thought of Penny.

'Do you think she'd consider coming to the Hall? She could be your physio as well as help out with all the administration.'

It seemed a lot to ask, to leave a good job and move away from friends to an unknown place, but to our surprise Penny responded warmly to the suggestion. She promised to think it over, and pray about it. A few weeks later she phoned, the decision made.

'I think it's right for me to come.'

In September she joined the staff of the Hall. Her presence made the world of difference. She took in hand my muddled correspondence, the planning of conferences and all the little day to day demands of running the Hall. In the very areas I needed support, she provided it. She even elected to remember people's birthdays for me, but in this her efficiency failed. After about the third forgotten birthday, I hit on the bright idea of purchasing a store of 'Sorry I'm late' cards which were liberally used from then on.

Hours were spent on my physiotherapy too. Penny was determined to see me walking properly, and finally our combined efforts yielded a marked improvement.

God was giving me every support. With Penny, I had both the encouragement and the practical help I had needed. I should have been satisfied.

But somehow I wasn't.

# CHAPTER 12

Sue was out at a parents' evening at the school. Ben had taken ages to get to sleep, and my 'babysitting role' had tired me out. Back in the kitchen, a little lonely, I decided to make myself a cup of cocoa to cheer myself up and keep away the early Autumn chill which was sneaking through my two thick woollies. I got out the milk, and spooned the cocoa carefully into a mug. Only a little spilt on to the table. Easy to slosh the milk into a saucepan, and then I had to light the gas.

It took me several seconds to unhook the gas lighter from its place beside the cooker. I could feel the irritation rising inside me as the lighter resolutely refused to let go its hold. A last, determined shake did the trick and I held it to the gas. Again and again I flicked the little button to raise a spark, but in vain. I turned off the gas in something approaching panic, afraid I might not be able to manage that either and Sue would come back to find me unconscious or even dead from the fumes.

I tried again, but no amount of effort would yield the necessary spark. Anger made my hand tremble and even less able to work the lighter. The pan of milk sat cold in front of me, almost in reproach. All it needed was a simple little flame. Finally, I brought the lighter down against the cooker with a crash, giving vent to my fury in calculated destruction. Again and again, coldly deliberate, I smashed the lighter until it lay in fragments at my feet.

Unseeing, I stared at the pieces for several seconds. I felt the anger drain out of my body, and at last I bent to clear up what I'd done.

A breath of fresh air with Sunny. That would clear my head, help me think. I called to her and limped out of the back door towards Happy Valley. I could feel my cheeks blazing hot, despite the evening coolness. Confused, upset, I couldn't believe I'd been so violently overwhelmed as to behave like a child with a tantrum. I was supposed to be an evangelist, telling others about Christ and encouraging them to commit their lives to Him. How could I presume to instruct them when I couldn't even control myself? I recoiled in horror from that part of me which had been so deliberately destructive. How could I ever preach another sermon after this?

I pretended everything was normal when Susie eventually returned. I couldn't even tell her what had happened, it shamed me too much.

Later, she found the broken pieces.

'I don't really know what happened,' I tried to explain. How could Sue be expected to understand when I couldn't understand myself? 'I couldn't light the gas, and suddenly I was furious.' Sue looked at me with the sympathy and concern I dreaded. I hated appearing so helpless, still prey to black moods and despair.

Guilt at my inability to cope consumed me at such times. Why couldn't I claim God's victory? Something was wrong and I didn't know how to put it right. Having got so far in my recovery, it was doubly frustrating to find there were still things I couldn't do. To all appearances, I was practically 'normal' once more, able to stand, walk, even drive and take conferences, but the truth was different: I was handicapped and couldn't get away from it. And time made it harder to accept, not easier.

People had asked me whether I ever thought of committing suicide when I lay paralysed in hospital. I could reply with complete honesty that it had never occurred to me. But now . . . Now, I found myself wondering whether I wouldn't be better off dead. I wasn't much of a husband any more, subjecting poor Susie to my moods and desolation and able to give her very little real assistance in running our home. I was horrified to find myself wondering, like John, why God had let me live after all. It would have been so much easier to have gone to the safety of heaven straight away.

'Did you really think you might die?' Noddy surprised me one evening.

I hesitated. 'Yes, yes I did.'

'Would you rather have gone to heaven?'

How could I be honest with her, and not seem ungrateful or unloving?

'Well, it would be lovely to be with Jesus, but I'd rather be with you.'

Noddy wrinkled her nose in scorn. 'Oh no you wouldn't. 'Course not.' I was taken aback at this straightforward appraisal. My eight-year-old daughter was giving me lessons in telling the truth.

'I mean,' I rallied, 'I mean, you might have missed me.'

'Yes,' Noddy looked down at the floor. 'We'd have been sort of glad and sad. Glad 'cos it would be lovely for you in heaven, and sad 'cos we'd miss you.'

Once again, God was using the words of a child to reassure me. 'Course I'd rather be in heaven. It was the goal we all strove towards, and nothing on earth would ever compare. But I needed to know more about how to manage the waiting time.

Then we heard that Joni, the author of the book that had meant so much to me, was coming to England. I could hardly believe it. My cousin was arranging her itinerary, and he asked if there was any chance of my fixing up some speaking engagements for her in the South. Was there! She could come to the Hall, visit Stoke, go to any number of lunch meetings and evening fellowships . . . Nick told me to slow down, Joni wouldn't be able to cover the whole of the South of England in a couple of days. But yes, a visit to the Hall and Stoke Mandeville sounded fine.

It was enough. I could hardly wait to meet this girl who felt like a friend just through the pages of her book. And to have her speak to my old buddies still trying to cope with their paralysis – it was marvellous.

I went to pick Joni up from Heathrow. Her plane was an hour late, but she didn't look at all tired or harassed when the ambulance eventually brought her to my car. Neither did her three travelling companions, her sisters Kathy and Jay, and her old school friend Betsy.

'Hi Max,' Joni greeted me warmly. Her smile was young, impish and pretty. I felt at ease with her at once.

'I've heard a lot about you,' Joni continued.

'I bet I've heard a lot more about you.'

She laughed and looked down at her hands. Her obvious embarrassment at being a well-known personality warmed me to her even more.

We edged out of Heathrow into Friday evening, rush-hour traffic. We would be late getting to Stoke. But a few minutes of conversation with Joni assured me we weren't going to find the journey too long. There was such a lot to share.

'So you broke your neck too, huh?' Joni began. I told her briefly about the accident, and how I'd been paralysed.

'But my, look at you now!' Her voice was admiring. 'Can you feel and move almost everything?'

I explained my 'split personality', aware all the time that she was watching me closely. I began to wonder if she was worried about my capabilities at the wheel with a partially paralysed right arm and leg, but in fact she was observing just how much I'd recovered.

'Your triceps aren't too strong, are they?' she commented. 'You're moving the wheel from your shoulder.' She was right. 'How do you grip?'

'My right thumb works a little, but it's my left hand I'm using mainly.'

'How's the sensation in your hands?'

I was surprised at the extent of her interest. She must have met dozens of handicapped people since her own accident eleven years before, yet she asked questions as if it was all new to her.

'Both my hands are about the same,' I answered. 'I can feel my thumb and forefinger almost normally, but each finger gets progressively worse until I can't tell I've got a little finger at all – I'm always shutting it in doors and things.'

'Yeah,' was the warm response. 'That's what my hands are like too.'

I felt the same reassurance talking to her as I'd felt reading her book, knowing she understood my situation because she'd travelled the same path.

'You know, Max,' she said gravely, 'You're one in a thousand. I've only ever met seven or eight people who've recovered like you.'

I didn't know what to say, conscious of her own complete paralysis. Her words made me realise the blessing I'd received as if I'd never realised it before. She had a wonderful way of making whoever she was with appreciate all that God had given, whether it had seemed good or bad before. It was a gift, and I noticed it time and again as I heard her speak to people. Travelling with her in the car, I felt worthwhile, wanted, valuable.

At Stoke, she held everyone spellbound. You could have heard a pin drop in that packed audience as she unfolded the story of her accident, explaining that after months of anger, bitterness and frustration, she came to trust God to weave the tapestry of her life.

Then Joni interrupted her talk to ask for a sketch pad. It was set up in front of her and, telling us how she'd been particularly encouraged to develop her art since she'd broken her neck, Joni took a pen in her mouth and began to draw.

'I see God as the master artist,' she said as she sketched. 'He wants to paint a beautiful picture with the canvas of our lives.' Her sister Kathy held up the sketch pad to show us the progress so far, revealing a cosy little Swiss chalet on a mountain side. There were murmurs of appreciation, and one or two gasps from those who realised the speed at which she worked.

Back to the drawing, and Joni explained that sometimes God appeared to be painting great big ugly lines which we could not understand. Her head jerked forwards in a flurry of fair hair as she manoeuvred the pen and drew two apparently random lines across the pad. Kathy held the result up.

'You may think I've ruined the picture now. But this is where you've got to trust that I know what I'm doing. Those lines are there for a purpose.'

A couple of minutes later, Kathy held up the finished product. Those ugly lines had been used as the trunks of two solid towering pine trees. Smiles spread across every face as the powerful point of her illustration sank in. It was all the more powerful because her own smile was proof that the Master Artist had done something in her life that was beyond dispute.

Joni's visit was a tremendous encouragement for me. Nonetheless I was awed by the way she seemed to cope so well with her situation. I couldn't imagine her breaking anything in helpless frustration like I had done. It wasn't until I visited her the following year in the States that I learnt we weren't so different after all.

At the time of my visit, Joni's book was being made into a film. To my amazement, Joni was acting her own part herself.

'Isn't it harrowing to go through it all again?' I couldn't help asking. We were sitting having supper in a cosy, wood-panelled room with a log fire crackling in the background.

'You bet it is.' Joni looked paler than I remembered, and tired.

'It's funny, you know, but all the old frustration has come

back again. I thought I'd dealt with it, but the filming has made me realise it's still there under the surface.'

Her admission encouraged me to talk about my own continuing frustration, sometimes so strong it overwhelmed me. I told her about breaking the gas lighter.

'But it's only human to have feelings, Max,' Joni returned gently. 'It's what we do with them that's important.'

'But I just don't know what to do with them.' My voice sounded despairing.

'Tell the Lord about them. We're made in His image after all so He's bound to understand.'

It seemed so simple put like that. I saw that Joni wasn't consumed by guilt at feeling angry or depressed. She realised such feelings were normal.

'We just have to keep bringing them back to Him,' she emphasised.

There was nothing super-spiritual about that. It was sensible, down to earth, and yet bang in the centre of God's will. I felt as if a huge burden had been lifted from my shoulders. All God asked of me was that I walk with Him, sharing my life totally. He wasn't going to take away my humanity. That was part of being alive in the world.

'But it's so *hard* sometimes,' I cried feelingly.

'Oh yes, yes it is,' Joni nodded, her eyes sad. 'I get homesick for heaven too.'

She understood. I hadn't expressed my longing for heaven in so many words, but she'd sensed it because it was her own experience too. I felt a rush of gratitude that I wasn't alone in wanting to be alive in eternity rather than on earth. So that was natural too. As I thought on in the quietness of Joni's sitting room, I realised our mutual longing was also thoroughly biblical. Hadn't Paul written about wanting to be with Christ rather than 'alive in the flesh'? 'My desire is to depart and be with Christ, for that is far better.' (Philippians 1:23). I'd never appreciated exactly what he'd meant by that until now. Before, life had been too good for me to set my eyes on heaven. Through my accident, God had reminded me where my proper home was, just as He had done with Joni. Later, I read in her second book, *A Step Further*:

> This life is not for ever. Nor is it the best life that will ever be. The good things here are merely images of the better things we will know in heaven ... Just as my artwork pleasantly but imperfectly reflects the nature I see, so this earth that we know is only a preliminary sketch of the glory that will one day be revealed. Reality – the final painting – lies in heaven.

A wonderful message sent by Corrie ten Boom reinforced the lesson Joni taught me. This gracious Dutch lady, who'd been through so much at the hands of the Nazis during the war, had travelled everywhere testifying to the love and forgiveness of the Lord. She was concerned for everyone who was suffering, and always had a word of kindness or encouragement based on her unshaken faith in God. She sent me a copy of her book, *He Cares, He Comforts* and directed me to a verse in the Bible.

> 'I consider that the sufferings of this present time are not worth comparing with the glory that is to be revealed to us.'
>
> Romans 8:18

So she too looked forward to heaven, and as I meditated on that verse I realised 'the sufferings of this present time' didn't merely refer to some specific trouble but the whole trauma of living in a fallen world. Life on earth would never be perfect. It was no good my thinking I could recover from the accident to an extent where nothing was wrong or unsatisfactory. That would only be the case in heaven. Life was a stepping stone to that perfection, a halfway point.

A letter accompanied Corrie's book. Pam, an old friend and Corrie's assistant, wrote:

> One thing I have seen anew this year is the fact that however valuable experience is, it is the grace of God

which enables us to live and work for Him from day to day. Experience helps us as we face new challenges which the Lord gives, but it does not carry us through. His grace does.

How that came home to me too. I knew I was guilty of thinking my harrowing experience and God's special care for me might have changed my old self, made me somehow 'holier'. My confusion and sense of inadequacy stemmed partly from a recognition that I hadn't changed one bit. I was still the same old sinful me, and it appalled me. I felt as if I was letting God down, after all He'd given me.

Pam's letter gently reminded me that I would never be in any other position than dependent on God's grace. I needed to rely on Him now just as much as I'd relied on Him in hospital. I wasn't more self-sufficient just because I could walk. I'd been trying to show myself and everyone that I could manage, but I was forgetting that nothing was achieved outside His grace.

'My grace is sufficient for you, for my power is made perfect in weakness.'

2 Corinthians 12:9

I was awed by how much God's power had manifested itself in my life. When I walked, however shakily, down to Happy Valley, or played with the children, I remembered the night in Exeter when I thought I'd never enjoy such simple pleasures again.

'Do you think you're a miracle?' people often asked me. I used to hedge the question a bit, saying that medically my recovery wasn't very special. It just didn't happen every day. Then James Jones challenged me.

'I'd say you were a miracle, Max. Undoubtedly.'

'But a miracle to me means that God bends the rules,' I protested. 'I don't think He did that for me.'

'But God's not bound to any rules,' James continued. 'He makes them.'

I tried to see what he was getting at.

'Your recovery was an answer to thousands of prayers wasn't it?' I nodded. 'Well, to me that's a miracle. Believing prayer rewarded against apparently overwhelming odds.'

I could see that. God had answered prayer in a wonderful way. Even though He'd worked through human channels, through doctors and my own physical, natural recovery, He'd wrought a miracle. An amazing miracle, the brightest and most beautiful flower on our rubbish dump.

And God again used the words of a child to remind me when that miracle would be perfected. We were round an evening fire at home, Annie on my knee and Noddy at my feet, and Ben nearly asleep in Sue's arms.

'If I'm naughty, you can't run after me and catch me,' Annie was telling me gleefully.

Noddy looked up. 'In heaven,' she said seriously, as if there was something Annie had overlooked, 'Daddy will get a new pair of legs.'

'Oh dear,' Annie put her finger in her mouth and her other arm round my neck. 'Well I better be good in heaven then.'

\*    \*    \*    \*    \*    \*

This is an unfinished story. Like every disciple of Jesus Christ, I am on a journey home and there is still further to go.

I would not be honest if I did not tell you that there are many hills on my own road that I have not yet learned to climb. But because of the guarantees of God's Word I am convinced that these difficulties on the journey are to prepare us for arriving home.

With this conviction, every day becomes an exciting amalgam. Glimpses of the panoramic view of our final destination mix with the struggles of scaling today's mountain.

We are halfway to heaven but still travelling. One day we shall be able to enjoy all that it means to be there.